WHO WROTE THAT?

Mythmaker: The Story of J. K. Rowling

Charles J. Shields

Chelsea House Publishers
Philadelphia

CHELSEA HOUSE PUBLISHERS

EDITOR IN CHIEF Sally Cheney
DIRECTOR OF PRODUCTION Kim Shinners
CREATIVE MANAGER Takeshi Takahashi
MANUFACTURING MANAGER Diann Grasse

STAFF FOR MYTHMAKER: THE STORY OF J. K. ROWLING

ASSOCIATE EDITOR Benjamin Kim
PICTURE RESEARCHER Jane Sanders
PRODUCTION ASSISTANT Jaimie Winkler
SERIES AND COVER DESIGNER Keith Trego
LAYOUT 21st Century Publishing and Communications, Inc.

http://www.chelseahouse.com

First Printing

1 3 5 7 9 8 6 4 2

Library of Congress Cataloging-in-Publication Data

Shields, Charles J., 1951–
    Mythmaker : the story of J. K. Rowling / by Charles J. Shields.
        p.   cm. — (Who wrote that?)
Includes bibliographical references and index.
    ISBN 0-7910-6719-X
 1. Rowling, J. K.—Juvenile literature. 2. Authors, English—20th century—
Biography—Juvenile literature. 3. Potter, Harry (Fictitious character)—
Juvenile literature. 4. Children's stories—Authorship—Juvenile literature.
I. Title. II. Series.
PR6068.093 Z884 2002
823'.914—DC21   2002000344

Table of Contents

7P 5FA

34027

J. K. Rowling in the "Hogwarts Express" on a four-day promotional tour for Harry Potter and the Goblet of Fire *that would take her up through Britain. The phenomenal success of her Harry Potter series has led to such extravagant promotional campaigns such as renting this vintage steam engine for $22,000 a day.*

Wild About Harry

He'll be famous—a legend—I wouldn't be surprised if today was known as Harry Potter day in the future—there will be books written about Harry—every child in our world will know his name!"

— Professor McGonagall in
Harry Potter and the Sorcerer's Stone

JUST SECONDS AFTER midnight London time on Friday, July 7, 2000, a 12-year-old boy named Louis Shulz purchased the first copy of *Harry Potter and the Goblet of Fire*, J. K. Rowling's fourth book in the series, at the six-story Waterstone's bookstore in the city's Picadilly neighborhood. Behind him, a line of 500 adults and children waited their turn, many clutching sleeping bags for an all-night celebration hosted by the store.

On the other side of the Atlantic Ocean as Friday evening drifted toward midnight in the United States, bookstore owners and staff peeked excitedly out the windows of their stores at crowds of Potter fans growing larger.

"I have never seen anything like this," Richard Klein, co-owner of Book Revue in Huntington, N.Y. had remarked earlier in the week in a *New York Times* article headlined "Harry Potter Book Becoming a Publishing Phenomenon."

"People are frenzied out there about this book," he said.

"The anticipation is beyond anything we imagined," agreed Michael Jacobs in the same article, a senior vice president at Scholastic, Rowling's American publisher. "The book has crossed over and is now being read by adults now as well as children. The anticipation has allowed us to have the biggest first printing in the history of trade publishing."

As the minutes ticked away, FedEx workers across the country loaded 9,000 trucks with 250,000 copies of *Harry Potter and the Goblet of Fire* pre-ordered through Amazon.com and destined to arrive on Saturday. At Point O'Pines Camp in Brant Lake, N.Y., a staff member asked the 300 girls at dinner-time how many expected to received a copy of Rowling's new book in the mail. About a third raised their hands.

But most of the 3.8 million printed were already stacked in bookstores, safeguarded by owners who had signed a legally binding pledge to Scholastic not to sell any copies before the midnight kick-off. "If we hear of any substantiated case of selling the books early, that bookseller will receive no subsequent shipments of Harry Potter books," said Scholastic's Jacobs. "I think everyone realizes that the stakes are high." Another two million copies were slated for printing later in the month.

Outside of the Upper West Side Barnes and Noble bookstore in Manhattan, 350 people—many of whom had been waiting since 10 P.M.—tugged their jackets and sweaters tighter in the unseasonably cool air. Inside the store, staffers adjusted their wizard costumes and checked the dry ice smoking silently in cauldrons beneath plastic spiders and star-shaped balloons hanging from the ceiling. Near the cash registers, six-foot pyramids of

Did you know...

At one point, the first three Harry Potter hardcovers and a paperback version of *Harry Potter and the Sorcerer's Stone* held the top spots on *The New York Times* best-seller lists in 1999 and 2000. As a result, the 68-year-old list introduced its first new offshoot in 16 years by creating a separate category for best-selling children's books. On July 23, 2000, a best-seller list of children's titles appeared. Some authors and publishers said that treating popular children's literature differently was not a compliment. Others said it was right to give special attention to the books, and the authors, preferred by young people.

books, each one an earlier title in the Potter series, stood ready to be rapidly dismantled. Eighteen million copies had already been sold in Britain and the United States since the appearance of the first book, *Harry Potter and the Sorcerer's Stone*, in 1998. Behind the counter lay all the copies of the coveted fourth book.

At the Borders bookstore in Santa Fe, N.M. a trio of jugglers arrived to entertain the waiting crowd. A thousand miles north at Tattered Cover in Denver, the staff blended a batch of ginger ale, apple cider, and dry ice to imitate Harry's favorite drink, butter beer.

Midnight drew near. At Books of Wonder in Manhattan, annoyed adults told half-a-dozen camera crews to back off and stop pushing the kids.

On the stroke of twelve, the news ticker in Times Square announced that *Harry Potter and the Goblet of Fire* was available in bookstores. Susan Scioli, owner of Community Bookstore in Brooklyn, drew back a curtain covering the storefront, snapped open the lock on the front door, and a witch ran out merrily ringing a gong.

By 12:15 A.M., Scioli had sold out her entire allotment of 580 copies of the book—500 of which had been pre-ordered and reserved by the customer's last name.

Did you know...

Amazon.co.uk, the British subsidiary of Amazon.com, the online bookseller, said advance orders of 400,000 copies of *Harry Potter and the Goblet of Fire* made it the biggest seller in its so far brief history of online bookselling.

Harry Potter fans—some wearing the trademark glasses—excitedly discuss their purchase of Harry Potter and the Goblet of Fire at a midnight sale in Calabasas, California.

In Britain, the sun was just coming up. The Hogwarts Express, carrying 34-year-old J.K. Rowling, was preparing to pull away from special platform 9 3/4 in King's Cross Station, London—the same spot from which Harry Potter had embarked to find his destiny at the Hogwarts School of Witchcraft and Wizardry. The vintage steam train, the oldest in Britain, had once been used by royalty. But now Rowling's British publisher, Bloomsbury, was renting it for $22,000 a day to bear the reigning queen of children's writers on a four-day promotional tour, up through England to Perth, Scotland. In the dining car, white linen and crystal covered the tables. Rowling told reporters she didn't feel like a celebrity, drawing smiles of disbelief. "I'd really love to talk to some children, if I ever manage to finish with you lot."

But time was short and Rowling posed for a final picture, leaning out of one of the passenger car windows. As the train left the station, crowds of adults and children who had come to see her off waved goodbye. In a sense, the colorful scene was not only about the publication of the latest Potter book, but also a celebration of children reading.

"I never thought I would say this, but for the first time I'm grateful to 'Harry Potter,' " said Craig Virden, the publisher of Random House Children's Books. Random House's sales of children titles rose by 12 percent in 1999 and rose still higher in 2000. "I think 'Harry Potter' has made reading cool," said Virden. "The best advertisement you can have is a kid talking to another kid about a book."

Rowling's first book, *Harry Potter and the Sorcerer's Stone*, had spent 14 weeks on the *New York Times* best-seller list. The only other children's title to come close to that mark was E.B. White's *Charlotte's Web*, which

Did you know...

Rowling is concerned about Harry Potter becoming over-commercialized. "I would do anything to prevent Harry from turning up in fast-food boxes everywhere," she told a *New York Times* writer. "I would do my utmost. That would be my worst nightmare."

Another Harry Potter fan begins reading immediately at a midnight sale of Harry Potter and the Goblet of Fire *as Barnes and Noble employees, also dressed for the occasion, look on.*

had logged three weeks in 1952. The ripple created by Harry's popularity reached other publishers of children's books almost immediately. All seven titles of C.S. Lewis's *Chronicles of Narnia* series, published in 1950, doubled in sales in 2000. Sales of Lloyd Alexander's *Chronicles of Prydian* series about Taran, the assistant pig keeper, tripled. Brian Jacques' *Redwall* books spiked suddenly as well.

Booksellers and librarians took note. Recognizing the hunger of Potter-starved readers awaiting the fourth Rowling book, Joseph-Beth Booksellers in Cincinnati started a Harry Potter Withdrawal Club, regaling its members with read-alouds from L. Frank Baum's *The Wizard of Oz*, and *The Book of Three*, Alexander's first title in the *Chronicles of Prydian* series. In public libraries nationwide, printed lists assuring young readers, "If you like Harry Potter, you'll like these, too. . . ." found their way into eager hands.

But now at last, the fourth book was out. On Saturday morning, July 8, planes flying above beaches in Los Angeles, Chicago, New York, New Jersey, and Hilton Head, N.C. towed banners in the summer sky proclaiming, " 'Harry Potter and the Goblet of Fire.' Read it Now!" Over the weekend, Barnes & Noble bookstores sold a half million copies; Borders bookstores, a quarter of a million more; and Amazon.com an additional 26,000. Random House/Listening Library released the largest printing of an audiobook children's title ever— 200,000 cassettes and CDs—of Jim Dale reading *Harry Potter IV*.

As the Hogwarts Express clanked noisily into stations, youngsters clutching vouchers from British booksellers

Did you know...

Jim Dale's audiobook narration of *Harry Potter IV* from Random House/Listening Library debuted at the same time as Rowling's fourth book. The first printing, which included both cassette and CD formats, was 200,000, the largest ever for a children's audiobook title, according to *Publisher's Weekly* magazine.

climbed aboard to meet the young woman whom newspapers claimed was third among Britain's top-earning women, and whom Queen Elizabeth had recently elevated to an Officer of the British Empire.

What is she like, this dedicated writer in whose imagination Harry Potter had suddenly appeared ten years earlier while she was looking out the window during a train ride to King's Cross station?

J. K. Rowling at the Glamour Magazine Women of the Year Awards in New York City. Describing herself as a "plain young girl" when she was growing up, Rowling is now a reluctant celebrity and uncomfortable with the glare of the public spotlight.

2

"A Freckly Little Girl"

A scarlet steam engine was waiting next to a platform packed with people. A sign overhead said Hogwarts Express, eleven o'clock. Harry looked behind him and saw a wrought-iron archway where the barrier had been, with the words Platform Nine and Three-Quarters *on it. He had done it.*

— from *Harry Potter and the Sorcerer's Stone*

J.K. ROWLING'S STORY begins, like that of her famous character, Harry Potter, at King's Cross railway station in London where her parents met in the early 1960s.

It was there—in one of England's largest terminals, built of iron and glass at the height of steam-powered trains in the mid-19th century—that Peter Rowling, 19, an automotive engineer for Rolls Royce, saw a young passenger who caught his eye. Her name was Anne, also 19. She was a lab technician of French and Scottish ancestry. After a courtship that lasted a year, Peter proposed to her—on another train!

Their first daughter, J. K. (Joanne Kathleen) Rowling was born July 31, 1966 near the city of Bristol at Chipping Sodbury General Hospital, "which I think is appropriate for someone who collects funny names," she commented later in a short autobiographic sketch titled "The Not Especially Fascinating Life of J.K. Rowling." A second daughter, Di was born two years later. The family lived in Yate, a small village to the west of Chipping Sodbury.

The Rowlings were affectionate parents. When Jo, as family and friends nicknamed her, came down with measles at age four, her father read to her from Kenneth Grahame's *Wind in the Willows*. This book, about a series of humorous adventures involving small animals, begins, "The Mole had been working very hard all the morning, spring-cleaning his little home. First with brooms, then with dusters; then on ladders and steps and chairs, with a brush and a pail of whitewash; till he had dust in his throat and eyes, and splashes of whitewash all over his black fur, and an aching back and weary arms."

The experience must have made an impression. Jo invented a story about her sister Di falling down a rabbit-hole and living on strawberries provided by the rabbit family. Then at five or six, she wrote a story about a rabbit with the measles whose friends come by for visits, including a giant Miss Bee. "Rabbits loomed large in our early story-telling sessions; we badly wanted a rabbit," Rowling said in her autobiographical sketch. "And ever since Rabbit and Miss Bee, I have wanted to be a writer, though I rarely told anyone so. I was afraid they'd tell me I didn't have a hope."

About that time, the family moved to the village of Winterbourne on the other side of Bristol. Jo and Di made friends with playmates in the neighborhood—a brother and sister named Ian and Vicki Potter. Jo liked the sound of "Potter" (her name is pronounced like "bowling," which inspired jokes at school about Jo "Rolling Pins"). Ian Potter led the girls in hijinks that the strait-laced Jo found thrilling— putting garden slugs on picnic plates, booby-trapping the training wheels on Vicki's bike, and daring the girls to run through wet cement, which they did.

When Jo was eight, her mother gave her a book that had been one of Mrs. Rowling's favorites as a child: Elizabeth Goudge's *The Little White Horse*. Goudge was a writer who in some ways mirrored what Rowling would become. She was an outstanding writer of children's stories, which often included magic spells, magic gates, long-lost relatives, and dazzling coincidences. Moreover, Goudge's writing was vivid and filled with strong visual images that conjure up a real world. Here's a scene, for instance, from *The White Witch*:

Whenever she returned to it Froniga found fresh delight in her home. When she got up on fine mornings she would find her window covered with frost flowers, behind them the fires of the rising sun. She could not see the sun, she could only see the flame that seemed sparkling and crackling just behind her window, and she would stretch out her arms and laugh with joy. The fire on her hearth had never seemed to burn so merrily. The apple logs had blue and yellow flames, the cherry logs smelt like flowers and the burning fir cones were edged with the same color that had sparkled behind the frost flowers on her window. She would kneel before the hearth, warming her hands and singing, and Pen her white cat would weave round and round her purring and vibrating. But Pen was not so white as the snowflakes that fell outside her window, sometimes singly, like the feathers of a white swan that had passed overhead, sometimes in dense masses of falling light. Her room too was then so full of light that the flames on the hearth paled and did not come into their own again until dark came and she drew the curtains, and sat with her spinning wheel before the fire.

Goudge's *The Little White Horse*, set in 1842, tells the story of 13-year-old Maria Merryweather. Her father's

Did you know...

The Andrew Carnegie Medal is presented annually to an outstanding book for young people published in the United Kingdom. Carnegie (1835-1919) was a Scots-born American industrialist who spent $56 million during the late 19th century to build 2,509 public libraries in the English-speaking world. In 1946, J. K. Rowling's favorite author as a child, Elizabeth Goudge, was awarded the Carnegie Medal for *The Little White Horse*. Fifty-one years later, Rowling was recommended for the same honor for *Harry Potter and the Philosopher's Stone* (the title of *Harry Potter and the Sorcerer's Stone* in Britain).

debts have taken away the London home she loved so much. Now there is only enough money to send Maria, her dog Wiggins, and her governess, Miss Heliotrope, to live with a mysterious, distant cousin, Sir Benjamin at Moonacre Manor. By solving a series of mysteries, Maria unravels the secrets behind her new home.

Of all the books Rowling read as a child, *The Little White Horse* remained her favorite. "[Goudge] always said exactly what the characters were eating. I found that really satisfying. That's why you always get lists of food at Hogwarts," she said. Also on her personal list of all-time favorites is *Manxmouse* by Paul Gallico ("It's superb"); *A Girl of the Limberlost* by Gene Stratton-Porter ("It freaked me out, because the father drowns in a swamp hole. But it's a magnificent book"); *Ballet Shoes* by Noel Streatfeild ("It's a very girly book. I still reread it"); Kenneth Grahame's *Wind in the Willows*, and C.S. Lewis' *The Chronicles of Narnia*.

In 1974 when Jo was nine, the Rowlings moved about 40 miles from Winterbourne to the tiny village of Tutshill, in the Wye river valley near England's border with Wales. The Rowling parents had been raised in London, and living in the country was one of their dreams.

The Wye valley, a little more than 100 miles from London, is a remarkably beautiful part of England. The poet William Wordsworth, vacationing near the river in the summer of 1798, was moved to write about "These waters, rolling from their mountain-springs/With soft inland murmur," and "steep and lofty cliffs" that "connect/ The landscape with the quiet of the sky." Within 20 miles of Tutshill are Tintern Abbey, one of the most romantic-looking ruins in Britain, Chepstow Castle, and Raglan Castle—all likely to impress the imagination of a child like

Rowling. She recalls that she and her sister were allowed to roam the banks of the Wye, and explore the southern-most part of the Royal Forest of Dean, which covers the valley like a green scarf.

The Forest of Dean is centuries old and was originally set aside for royal hunting. Later, timber from the forest was used to fuel iron furnaces of the Industrial Revolution and to supply the British navy with masts, yardarms, and planks. In 1938, the government desig-nated it a National Forest Park, the first in England. Parts of the forest are quite remote, accessible by lonely roads and footpaths. Perhaps Rowling was thinking of the Forest of Dean when she described the Forbidden Forest in *Harry Potter and the Sorcerer's Stone:* "[Hagrid] led them to the very edge of the forest. Holding his lamp up high, he pointed down a narrow, winding earth track that disappeared into the thick black trees. A light breeze lifted their hair as they looked into the forest."

School, on the other hand, was a disappointment. On her first morning at Tutshill Primary, Rowling took a test on fractions and failed it. The teacher, she said, had the pupils divided into "smart" rows on the left and "stupid" rows on the right. The new girl who couldn't do fractions ended up "as far right as you could get without sitting in the playground." Eventually, the teacher ordered Jo to swap seats with her best friend in a left row, which ended up hurting their friendship.

Rowling described herself at 11 as a "freckly little girl" who was "short, squat, [with] very thick National Health glasses—free glasses that were like bottle bottoms—that's why Harry wears glasses. I was shy. I was a mixture of insecurities and very bossy. Very bossy to my sister but quite quiet with strangers. Very bookish. Terrible at school. That whole thing about Harry being able to fly so well is probably total wish fulfillment." Still, from this contradictory mixture of traits, she later created her second most memorable character after Harry Potter—Hermione Granger. From the instant Hermione marches into the train compartment where Harry and Ron Weasley are sitting, Rowling paints a portrait of a take-charge girl:

> "Has anyone see a toad? Neville's lost one," she said. She had a bossy sort of voice, lots of bushy brown hair, and rather large front teeth.

Rowling said Hermione is based pretty solidly on herself at 11. "She is really a caricature of me," Rowling explained. "I wasn't as clever as she is, nor do I think I was quite such a know-it-all, though former classmates might disagree. Like Hermione, I was obsessed with

Did you know...

Rowling borrowed the last name of her childhood friends in Winterbourne, Ian and Vicki Potter, for her main character. Ian Potter recalls how the three of them loved to play dress-up. "And nine times out of ten," he said, "it would be Joanne who had the idea, and she'd always say, 'Can't we be witches and wizards?'" Mr. Potter said he has read all of his famous friend's books aloud to his own children.

achieving academically, but this masked a huge insecurity. I think it is very common for plain young girls to feel this way."

But Rowling could not rely on her own school experiences to create Hogwarts, however, a setting that tests the cleverness and stamina of all her characters. "I'm often asked whether I went to boarding school and the answer is 'no.' I went to a 'comprehensive'—a state-run day school. I had no desire whatsoever to go to boarding school (though if it had been Hogwarts, I would have been packed in a moment)."

Her parents enrolled her at Wyedean Comprehensive at about the same age that Harry started at Hogwarts. She must have felt a little apprehensive, having heard the same rumor about Wyedean that Dudley tells Harry about Stonewall High about schoolkids taking the new students' heads and putting them in the toilet. But it turned out to be a traditional myth meant to make new kids nervous, and Rowling soon settled in. She entertained friends during lunch with long stories that unfolded every day in which each of them faced down some incredible challenge and won—later a key story element in all her books. One of her listeners and most devoted friends was a classmate named Sean Harris, who became the model for Ron Weasley.

As it turned out, falling back on her own courage was necessary when the toughest girl in her class picked a fight with her. "I didn't have a choice, she started hitting me and it was hit back or lie down and play dead. For a few days I was quite famous because she hadn't managed to flatten me. The truth was that my locker was right behind me and held me up. I spent weeks afterwards peering nervously around corners in case she was waiting to ambush me."

She found, however, a fighter of a different sort she could take as her own hero. Someone whose strength, independence, and opinions she could admire—an English journalist named Jessica Mitford. As teenagers, both Joanne and Di were attracted to social causes, but only in a showy way "We were that kind of, 'I'm the only one who really feels these injustices. No one else understands the way I feel.' I think a lot of teenagers go through that." But then when she was 14, her aunt told her about social activist Jessica Mitford. "'You know what she did, Jo,' her aunt said, "'she bought a camera on her father's account and then went travelling.'"

Jessica Mitford had been born into an aristocratic family, but came to believe that socialism—shared ownership of factories, mines, railroads, and land—would create a more just society, a view that offended her family. Traveling to Spain in the late 1930s to fight on the side of the Communists in the Spanish Civil War, Mitford met and married a soldier who was later killed in World War II. In the 1950s she broke off with the Communist Party when she could no longer support the policies of the Soviet Union. Instead, she put her energies into becoming a "muckracking" journalist—someone who investigates corruption and injustice. Her best-known book, *An American Way of Death* (1963), attacked the funeral industry for permitting greedy and deceptive practices. Rowling admired Mitford's political views, especially her determination to carry on despite terrible personal losses—the deaths of three of her children. "She had a total lack of self-pity," Rowling said. In *Harry*

Jessica Mitford, the English journalist whose socialist beliefs, independent lifestyle and inner strength were greatly admired by the teenaged J. K. Rowling.

Potter and the Goblet of Fire, she would pay tribute to Mitford by having Hermione defy authority and champion the rights of elves.

It was fortunate that Rowling found someone like Mitford to take as her ideal at 14. For also that year, in 1980, her mother Anne was diagnosed with multiple sclerosis.

J. K. Rowling at a press conference in Toronto. Although she is occasionally annoyed by the perception that she was penniless before finding success with her writing, she did in fact struggle through dull occupations whose only saving grace was the free time they allowed her to work on her books.

3

Harry Appears

"I'm a what?" gasped Harry.
"A wizard, o' course," said Hagrid, sitting back down on the
sofa, which groaned and sank even lower, "an' a thumpin'
good'un, I'd say, once yeh've ben trained up a bit."

—from *Harry Potter and the Sorcerer's Stone*

J. K. ROWLING'S mother Anne was 35 when she was diagnosed with multiple sclerosis, a disorder of the central nervous
system. When Joanne learned of her mother's condition, the
news must have hit her hard. "Because I was the older child,"

she said, "to me she was almost like an older sister. I was never in any doubt that she was my mum, but that kind of relationship was there. I could talk to her a lot more freely than some of my friends spoke to their mothers."

As part of her way of coping, Joanne created two identities: one to please her family, and one to please herself. On the one hand, she became head girl, or first in her class, at Wyedean Comprehensive, despite her statements later that she was a terrible student. Along with the honor came duties she didn't enjoy very much, but she accepted them. Once, she had to escort "Lady Somebody" around the school fair. Another time, she was asked to lead a school assembly. To pare down her role as master of ceremonies, she played a record instead—a plan which backfired, as the music kept skipping over and over. Joanne stood there mortified until the Head Mistress kicked the record player.

On the other hand, she discovered that adopting a more devil-may-care attitude suited her too, and probably helped conceal her fears about her mother. Now that she was wearing contact lenses instead of glasses, Joanne felt more confident. She discovered it was fun attracting disapproving looks from adults when she and some tough-looking boys in leather jackets shared cigarettes at the bus stop every

Did you know...

Rowling agreed with her parents that a job as a bilingual secretary might be interesting, and a good way to use her French degree. But she later said, "Unfortunately I am one of the most disorganized people in the world and, as I later proved, the worst secretary ever."

morning. She thought her idol, Jessica Mitford, the social activist who did things her way, would approve.

But there was no denying she was a good student. After graduating from Wyedean, she enrolled at the University of Exeter in the southwest corner of England—a selective school of 10,000 students with several branch campuses.

Her classes in the humanities met at the Streatham campus, the largest and busiest of the university's three sites, set on 245 hilly acres. A web site welcoming new students to Exeter boasts that the campus is "most beautiful in the country with loads of grass to loaf on, woods in which you can bond with trees and watch the squirrels, and gardens to wander aimlessly around." Again, Rowling pulled high marks. If she had any shortcomings academically, it was checking out library books and not returning them on time. Once, she ran up late fines totaling over $250. After paying off the charges, she did the same thing again.

In college, students must choose a major, and Rowling later confessed to choosing the wrong one. Her parents persuaded her to study French as a steppingstone to a career in international business. Her first love in school had always been English, although she had never confided her hopes of being a writer to any of her teachers. Now, faced with having to pursue a field of study for a degree, she went against her instincts and opted for French and Classics. She later advised some Harry Potter fans interviewing her in an Internet chat room not to follow her example, but listen to their own hearts when it came to making career choices. Nevertheless, as part of her studies, she dutifully went to Paris for a year to work as a teaching assistant. In 1987, she graduated from Exeter. At the ceremony, Anne Rowling watched from a wheelchair in the audience, noticeably worse in health than she had been six years before.

As a new graduate, the young French major started looking

for jobs and moved to London. The hope of becoming a writer still burned, and she went looking for a position where the work would be a good fit with her secret ambition. She accepted a job as a researcher and bilingual secretary with Amnesty International. Amnesty International champions the rights of political prisoners around the world, and Rowling found that in an office of thinkers and readers like herself, she could sneak time at her desk for creative writing now and then. During meetings, she doodled odd names in the margin of her legal pad such as "Dumbledore," a medieval word for bumblebee, and imagined what a character with such a name would be like.

But it was clear to her that she was just killing time with office work. She tried changing jobs, landing one as a secretary in Manchester this time. It was routine and involved mainly filing and typing, which she found tedious. Outside of work, she wrote for long hours, preferring to sit at a quiet table in a pub or cafe. She eventually completed one novel for adults and half of another, but she wasn't happy with either effort.

Then one day during a train ride from Manchester to London in 1990, she got an idea for a long, rich story that captivated her. The train trip should have been a short hop between cities, with a final stop at King's Cross station, but delays kept drawing out the journey. Rowling, feeling bored, stared out the train window at cows in a pasture. Suddenly, for no reason she can recall, Harry Potter "just sort of strolled" into her mind.

She said it was "the most incredible feeling" to suddenly have so much of this idea come to her. The character she envisioned, to whom unexplainable things kept happening, didn't know his own power. "I knew he was a wizard and he didn't know he was a wizard," she said of her first realization of Harry Potter's character. "And then it was a process of working backwards to find out how that could be, and forwards to find out what happened next."

The daydream-story enthralled her. Like a game, the tale could have hidden clues, formulas for spells, humorous and threatening characters—so much taking place during the education of a young wizard that more than one book would be needed to tell everything, beginning to end.

For the next four hours as the train ambled toward King's Cross, Rowling let her imagination play with the problem of how Harry Potter would become a wizard. First, something

Did you know...

An author rarely comes up with a completely original idea. Other authors have explored settings and characters similar to Rowling's. What matters is how a story develops, how well it's told, and what themes are treated. For example:

· *The Worst Witch* (1974) series by Jill Murphy for young readers (7-to-11-year-olds) is about Mildred, a student at Miss Cackle's Academy for Witches who does everything wrong. There are broom-riding lessons, animal helpers with minds of their own, scary teachers, potions gone wrong, and school uniforms that look like Halloween costumes.

· Diana Wynne Jones' *Witch Week* (1982) is a darkly funny suspense story about an outbreak of illegal magic in a school full of witch orphans—children whose parents have been burned as witches.

· Neil Gaiman's *The Books of Magic* (1990) features a dark-haired, bespectacled boy who discovers he's a wizard. He is accompanied by a magic owl.

· Rowling has said Harry Potter has a "spiritual ancestor"—Wart, the young King Arthur in T.H. White's *The Once and Future King*.

would have to distinguish him as exceptional—a lightening-shaped scar seemed right. Then he would be summoned to attend a boarding school for wizardry. A boarding school would be best because the characters would stay there at night, a perfect setting for magical goings-on. The school would be rather dreary and have ghosts, too. Thinking about ghosts, the characters Nearly Headless Nick and Peaves appeared to her full-blown. Another advantage of a boarding school would be that all the wizards-in-training would be among peers for months, free from interfering grown-ups save for their instructors in magic. And finally, the location of this school would be a mystery. Hidden from ordinary people, it would be in plain sight only to the select few who could enter through its enchanted doors.

When at last the train arrived in King's Cross Station—where platform 9 3/4 would become one day become as famous as the wardrobe in C.S. Lewis's *The Chronicles of Narnia*—the secret of Harry Potter and his world was Rowling's alone to write about. Returning to Manchester, she hoped none of her officemates would invite her to lunch so she could spend time by herself in pubs and cafes sketching out this story that absorbed her.

Besides helping to relieve the tedium of her office job a little, her inspiration may have come at a good time in her life for another reason. Earlier in the year at Christmastime, she had returned home to be with her family. Her mother's illness was quite advanced. Rowling tried to remain defiantly optimistic, denying that the end was near. "I can't believe in retrospect that I didn't really realize what was about to happen because she was so ill," she said later about her mother. "Her mobility was very limited; she looked ill, very ill— which I'd never really seen before. She was absolutely exhausted."

A few months later, in the spring of 1990, Rowling's

A bookstore in Munich showing Harry Potter posters. When inspiration struck Rowling, she had a firm idea of what Harry would look like, including his lightning-shaped scar and decidedly un-heroic appearance in general.

father went upstairs for a routine check on his wife. She had died, age 45, of respiratory failure.

"It was a huge shock," Rowling said. "I didn't expect it to be right round the corner. It was something about the fact that she was still very young. I just thought that she'd be around for years more, and . . . she wasn't." The loss of her mother would be difficult, but she would work through it by writing the first Harry Potter book in earnest in another country—Portugal.

The quays of Oporto, Portugal. Rowling ended up here after her mother died, and began work on the book that would become Harry Potter and the Philosopher's Stone. *While in Portugal, she had a brief marriage with journalist Jorge Arantes, and gave birth to a daughter, Jessica.*

4

Half a Suitcase of Stories

After all, to the well-organized mind, death is but the next great adventure.

—*Dumbledore in* Harry Potter and the Sorcerer's Stone

NINE MONTHS AFTER her mother's death, Rowling accepted a position abroad teaching English as a foreign language. "I really needed to get away. A lot of bad stuff had happened, and I needed to sort myself out a bit."

She went to Oporto, Portugal, a center of European trade

since the 12th century. Oporto sits on a sunny terraced slope rising from the Duoro River on Portugal's northern coast. Steeped in history from the days of the Portuguese empire, rich in architecture by the Romans, Moors, and Christian Crusaders, the tangled medieval side streets must have offered Rowling the change in scene she wished for.

She found it was fun teaching English to beginners, and laughed when her students gently teased their 26-year-old teacher about her last name, calling her Miss "Rolling Stone." Her hours were perfect, too—she worked afternoons and evenings, which left her mornings open for writing.

She buckled down to figuring out the extended storyline of Harry Potter. Even though the broad outline had occurred to her on the Manchester-to-London train, developing the intricacies of plot would take two years. Progress was glacially slow on the first book, *Harry Potter and the Philosopher's Stone* (changed to *Harry Potter and the Sorcerer's Stone* in the United States). She started the first chapter ten different ways, always in longhand, her preference for early drafts.

When journalists suggest to her that the reason she immersed herself in Harry Potter was because she wanted to escape from grieving about her mother's death, she takes offense. She points out that the inspiration for the story and the early work began six months before her mother's death. A hint of contradiction creeps in, however, when she admits that "Nothing was bigger than my mother dying," and that "Dealing with bereavement is a strong part of the books. Dealing with loss." Drawing on her own feelings of loss, in fact, Rowling produces one of the most memorable scenes in *Harry Potter and the*

Philosopher's Stone in Chapter 12, "The Mirror of Erised." Harry sees his long dead parents in a magic mirror:

> He looked in the mirror again. A woman standing right behind his reflection was smiling at him and waving. He reached out a hand and felt the air behind him. If she was really there, he'd touch her, their reflections were so close together, but he felt only air—she and the others existed only in the mirror. . . . The Potters smiled and waved at Harry and he stared hungrily back at them, his hands pressed flat against the glass as though he was hoping to fall right through it and reach them. He had a powerful kind of ache inside him, half joy, half terrible sadness.

"The mirror is almost painfully from my own feelings about my mother's death," Rowling told a reporter for *The Guardian* newspaper in Manchester, England. She added that if she were looking in the mirror she would see exactly

Did you know...

Rowling finds it amusing that myths have grown up about how poor she was when she was writing *Harry Potter and the Sorcerer's Stone*. "I had an American journalist say to me, 'Is it true you wrote the whole of the first novel on napkins?' I really wanted to say, 'No, on teabags. I used to save them.'"

She still has no car though, and likes to spend time at a coffee shop on the steep, winding medieval street in Edinburgh that was the inspiration for her tales' mystical shopping street, Diagon Alley.

what Harry saw. "I'd gabble on and at the end of five minutes I'd realize I hadn't asked what it's like to be dead. It's the selfishness of the child, isn't it?—at least I'm aware of that. But it couldn't be long enough."

But she wouldn't permit herself the needed time to grieve over her mother, either. Her attitude was "Let's keep going and keep moving." Hence she picked up and moved far away, and "That started this sort of train of mishaps and misadventures," she admitted later. Barely a year after arriving in Portugal, Rowling married journalist Jorge Arantes on October 16, 1992. In 1993, her daughter Jessica was born, named for Jessica Mitford, Rowling's real-life heroine. Not long after, however, the marriage disintegrated for reasons known only to Rowling and Arantes. Rowling puts a terse spin on the relationship, saying only "I got married. We got separated. We got divorced." Rowling usually changes the subject in interviews when her brief first marriage is brought up. Rowling left Portugal, taking Jessica with her. "It's a funny thing," she said, "but I doubt very much there would have been a Jessie if mum hadn't died when she did."

Now suddenly she was on her own—a single parent and temporarily jobless. She migrated to Edinburgh, Scotland at Christmastime to stay a few weeks with her sister Di. Her plan was to stay only long enough to figure out what to do next, but the city of Edinburgh began to charm her. Scotland's capital city looks like a theater backdrop to an 18th-century play. Church spires poke everywhere above the gray-brown stone buildings of the skyline. Steeply-built streets roll up and down green hillsides and meander through parks, and perched high above the city atop a rocky crag sits Edinburgh Castle, sections of which are 900 years old. Thinking strictly on a practical level, Rowling took into account the free museums, the manageability of the city's

A street in Edinburgh, Scotland. Rowling visited her sister here and decided that it would be a good city to settle in while she finished her novel and worked as a French teacher.

size, and the good public transportation. "'I'll have a much better life here on a low income with my daughter,'" she decided. "I could just see that broke single-parenthood here would be easier."

When she had left Portugal, half her suitcase was stuffed

"were papers covered with stories about Harry Potter." Now that she had found a good place for her and Jessica to settle, she vowed to finish the novel before starting work as a French teacher, and try to get it published.

As usual, she forced herself to be optimistic, even though her circumstances were hardly ideal for an unpublished writer. Mice would run out from under the furniture and scratch in the walls at night in the tiny, chilly apartment she rented. Public daycare centers had a policy of not taking babies, and no fulltime job paid enough to make private daycare affordable. For 18 months she relied on welfare payments, supplementing the money with income from part-time work. She felt lonely and frustrated but was determined to meet her self-imposed deadline of finishing her novel. Wheeling her daughter in a stroller through the streets of Edinburgh, she would stop somewhere for tea and write a little if Jessica fell asleep. "I could not afford the luxury of writer's block and so I wrote with intensity." A favorite haunt was Nicholson's Café because it was quiet.

Thoughts that she was letting her daughter down assailed her sometimes. A particularly bad moment came when she was visiting another mother with a baby boy about her daughter's age. The little boy had a bedroom full of toys. By comparison, "when I packed Jessica's toys away," Rowling said, "they fitted into a shoe box, literally. I came home and cried my eyes out." For months, a fit of depression clouded her thinking. Later, she personified the feeling with the Dementors, who suck all hope and good thoughts out of their victims in *Harry Potter and the Prisoner of Azkaban*.

But eventually, she found a typing job that paid a good wage. She squeezed in coursework that would earn her a teaching certificate in Scotland, too. The whole time no one knew she was working on a novel except her sister who encouraged her to keep on, and her ex-husband who knew she wrote. Just once she confided the secrets of her writing life to a friend. The woman responded by giving her an incredulous look like she had said she was going to solve her problems by winning the lottery.

In 1995, she finished *Harry Potter and the Philosopher's Stone*. All this time, she had made no contacts in the publishing world and enlisted no agent to represent her. From a directory of agents, she chose the Christopher Little Literary Agency in London because she liked the sound of the name. Unable to afford the cost of duplicating her 80,000-word original typed manuscript, she spent weeks typing a back-up copy for herself.

Then she mailed off three sample chapters of this novel she'd had worked on for five years to someone she'd never met, and waited.

It really was like hoping to win the lottery.

Rowling signs a copy of one of her Harry Potter books for essay contest winners in New York. Another unique promotional campaign involved the essay contest "How the Harry Potter Books Have Changed My Life."

5

Bidding War

"And some old witch in Bath had a book that you could never stop reading! *You just had to wander around with your nose in it, trying to do everything one-handed."*

— from *Harry Potter and The Chamber of Secrets*

EVERY AGENT AND publishing house has a stack of unrequested manuscripts called the slush pile. Sometimes real gems can be found in it—well-written, well-told stories that some undiscovered talent has submitted. But a manuscript by an unknown writer tends more often than not to be returned, provided a return envelope is included. If a return envelope isn't included, then the piece gets tossed in a wastebasket. A reply letter is sent which says, in effect, "Thanks, but no thanks."

Unknowingly, Rowling had put herself at a disadvantage with Christopher Little from the start. Her chances that he would want to be her agent were less than zero. He didn't even take on children's authors as clients. But through a fluke, her submission landed on the top of the slush pile. Her thick envelope got pulled off the heap, opened, and its contents were read.

Not long after, Rowling received a letter at her apartment in Edinburgh from the Christopher Little Literary Agency. Expecting a few sentences of rejection, she steeled herself to be disappointed—but instead, the letter said, "'Thank you. We would be pleased to receive the balance of your manuscript on an exclusive basis.'" Not only did this mean that Little was interested in her novel, but he wanted to make certain Rowling didn't show it to any of his competitors. She read the letter eight times in disbelief. Some authors get their books published without an agent. But for a first-timer like Rowling, having an agent can be a big advantage. An agent is supposed to know the publishing industry, guiding his or her client to the doorstep of the right publishing house. With Little helping her, Rowling had good reason to be excited. His offer meant that, as a professional, he believed in her as a writer.

Still, having an agent is just a first step. Little's job was to market the manuscript to various publishers, who may or may not think it's worth their time and money. Trusting in her agent, Rowling waited on pins and needles.

Meanwhile, she found a position teaching French in a

Scottish high school, now that her goal of finishing her novel had at last been met. Again, she was a hit with the students. In grade school, her nickname had been "rolling pins" like bowling pins. In Portugal, her students dubbed her Miss Rolling Stone. Now, she couldn't resist laughing when students serenaded her with the theme from the TV program *Rawhide*, singing "Rolling, rolling, rolling . . . keep those wagons rolling!" They also loved doing impressions of her English accent, which to their Scottish ears sounded drowsy and bored.

But there was a secret that Rowling kept private and didn't want anybody to know: that she was an aspiring writer hoping desperately to get published. One day, when a student announced she didn't have any paper to write with, Rowling gave her the usual warning and instructed her to tear a sheet out of the notebook on the teacher's desk. The girl lingered over the notebook for a minute, reading a page of her teacher's handwriting. "Miss, are you a writer?" she asked suddenly.

"No," Rowling answered, embarrassed at being found out. "It's just a hobby." In fact, she was already busy on a second Harry Potter novel—*Harry Potter and the Chamber of Secrets.*

But her agent Christopher Little wasn't having much luck at finding takers for *Harry Potter and the Philosopher's Stone*. Major publishers were turning it down, including HarperCollins and Penguin. One editor decided a story set in a boarding school probably wouldn't interest young readers because the setting was too strange. All the publishers who gave it thumbs down mentioned it was too long, too— hundreds of pages. What youngster would want to plough through a book like that when R.L. Stein's quickie Goosebumps titles sold millions of copies? From publisher's reactions, Rowling concluded that if her novel ever were

Rowling meets with Queen Elizabeth at Bloomsbury's offices in London. One of the highest honors for a citizen of the United Kingdom is to meet the queen.

to see the light of day, it wouldn't sell very well.

Then Little tried Bloomsbury Publishing, a small firm in London. Founded barely ten years earlier in 1986 by four entrepreneurs, Bloomsbury was on the lookout for rare finds. An editor at Bloombury dutifully scanned the opening page of Harry Potter and began to read on, passing chapters as they were read to colleagues around the office. The next day, Rowling received a call from her agent. "We've got a deal at Bloomsbury," Little told her. They were offering $3,600. Rowling joyfully accepted. For days she felt like she was walking on air, knowing that her book was actually going to be in stores.

There was a similar feeling at Bloomsbury. Company

president Nigel Newton remembered later that news about how "we have just bought the most extraordinary book" circulated throughout the office. One touchy issue remained to be addressed, however—how the author's name should appear on the cover. A female author might discourage boys. What about the initials "J.K." instead? Rowling, too happy to care about so small a detail at that point, agreed. Then, Bloomsbury contracted with Rowling to print a mere 500 copies of *Harry Potter and the Philosopher's Stone*—

Did you know...

Not everyone approved of the changes from British to American speech in *Harry Potter and the Sorcerer's Stone*. In an essay in the *New York Times* titled "Harry Potter, Minus a Certain Flavour," Peter Gleick complained:

> Do we really want children to think that crumpets are the same as English muffins? Frankly, reading about Harry and Hermione eating crumpets during tea is far more interesting to an American than reading about them eating English muffins during a meal. Are any books immune from this kind of devolution from English to 'American' English? Would we sit back and let publishers rewrite Charles Dickens or Shakespeare? I can see it now: 'A Christmas Song,' 'A Story of Two Cities,' 'The Salesman of Venice.' By protecting our children from an occasional misunderstanding or trip to the dictionary, we are pretending that other cultures are, or should be, the same as ours.

a number that seems especially comical now.

As the book opens, an evil wizard, Voldemort, has just the night before killed Harry's wizard and witch parents, James and Lilly Potter. He failed, however, to do away with the couple's one-year-old infant Harry, who somehow deflected Voldemort's awful powers. But the terrible encounter has left Harry with a lightning-shaped scar on his forehead. Friends of Harry's parents whisk away the now legendary child to safekeeping with his Muggle (non-magical) suburban middle-class aunt and uncle, Petunia and Vernon Dursley, and their bullying overweight son Dudley.

Ten years later, Harry is suffering through a lonely child-hood, forced to live in the cupboard under the stairs at the home of the Dursleys. He knows nothing about his heritage, or about his fame in the wizard world. The Dursleys punish him when he does anything out-of-ordinary, such as communicating in a friendly way with a snake at the zoo.

Then Hagrid, a huge messenger from the world of magic, confronts the Dursleys and invites Harry to enroll at Hogwarts School of Witchcraft and Wizardry. He takes the bewildered youngster shopping for school supplies such as a cauldron and wand, and offers the first sign of affection that Harry can remember. Uncle Vernon is outraged and tries to prevent Harry from pursuing his destiny.

Despite his uncle's protests, Harry departs for Hogwarts from platform Nine and Three-Quarters at London's King's Cross. On the train, Harry becomes acquainted with his soon-to-be best friend at Hogwarts, Ron Weasley.

Hogwarts has four houses for students—Gryffindor, Ravenclaw, Hufflepuff, and the sinister Slytherin. First-year students are placed into the appropriate house by a singing Sorting Hat. Harry's life takes an upturn when he finds he is a natural broomstick flyer. He is even picked for the

Two young readers dressed as Harry Potter reading in a bookstore. The level of fanaticism for the books has many readers adopting the look of the book's characters.

Gryffindor Quidditch team. Quidditch, a high-flying game with three kinds of balls and seven players per team, is rough and can result in injuries. Madam Pomfrey, the school nurse, cures with special spells and the magic of rest.

Harry's first year at Hogwarts is filled with adventure, friendship, and danger. He finds the Mirror of Erised, and mourns the loss of his parents when he sees them in the mirror's reflection. He finds he must be on guard against his own enemies too, such as Potions teacher Severus Snape and classmate Draco Malfoy. With his Gryffindor friends Ron Weasley and Hermione Granger, Harry undertakes a mission: to prevent the sorcerer's stone from falling into the hands of Voldemort and his allies. The stone offers eternal life and hence would be key to Voldemort's plans to return to power.

Now that *Harry Potter and the Philosopher's Stone* would be coming out, bookstore orders perked along but didn't break records. At the September 1997 Bologna Book Fair in Italy, Bloomsbury offered foreign publishing rights for one of their latest books by an unknown author named J. K. Rowling. Publishers sometimes hope to boost sales by reselling the rights to a book to other publishers in other countries.

Did you know...

Children's book illustrator Mary GrandPré is known for her memorable, haunting and dramatic work. Drawing Harry Potter for the American editions wasn't difficult, she said, because the author provides "rich visual information" about his appearance. In addition, GrandPré knew that Harry would attend Hogwarts over the course of seven books, so she decided early on to "Be true to him as his character changes and he grows up." That, said the St. Paul, Minnesota artist, in an interview with *USA Today*, is more about "how he carries himself, how he looks different from the inside out," than it is about his physical appearance. As Harry gains confidence, his smile grows wider with each cover.

Attending the fair was Arthur A. Levine, vice president of Scholastic Book Group, who was scouting the exhibition booths for fantasy titles that might do well in the United States. He picked up a complete, pre-print layout of Harry Potter and read it on the plane back to New York. The engaging, fast-paced, and imaginative story delighted him, with its themes of friendship, loyalty and courage holding the story together. Unfortunately, Levine was not alone in uncovering a winner. By the time he arrived in New York, nine other publishers were prepared to bid on rights to the book, and Bloomsbury found itself in the highly desirable position of conducting a spirited auction for a book it had purchased for only $3,600. Christopher Little phoned his client in Edinburgh and said her book was the contested prize between heavyweight publishers that included Hyperion, Putnam, Random House and Scholastic. Rowling assumed a few thousand dollars were at stake and waited patiently for the result.

Then the phone ran late at night in her apartment. On the line was Arthur Levine, still at his office in New York because of the five-hour time difference. He told her that Scholastic had successfully purchased the rights from Bloomsbury to publish *Harry Potter and the Philosopher's Stone* for $105,000—the highest amount ever paid for a foreign children's novel. "Don't be scared," he told her. She replied, "Thanks; I am."

Like a spell, feelings of disbelief clung to her for the next few days. "I was writing for me," she explained to the *Guardian* newspaper later. "For someone to offer that amount of money for something that I had written because it is the sort of thing I like reading was incredible." Her teaching contract having expired the previous summer, Rowling realized that now she didn't even have to substitute teach—

she could realize her dream of writing full-time.

Over the next few weeks, Levine enlisted Rowling's help in tailoring her novel for the children's book market in the United States. The phrase "philosopher's stone" in the title, for instance, would be better understood by Americans if it were "sorcerer's stone." Likewise, three kinds of changes were necessary to "Americanize" the text throughout. The first were spelling changes: "gray" for "grey," "color" for "colour," "pajamas" for "pyjamas," and so on. The second were differences in common words or phrases: "sweater" for "jumper," "taped" for "sellotaped," "mail" for "post," and so on. The third kind of change was a little trickier—finding American equivalents to English experiences. The English have crumpets for breakfast, for instance. Americans have, well, English muffins. Rowling could see the wisdom in all of this, as the plot, characters, and themes were more critical than anything else, so she agreed to the changes.

Then Levine got to work dressing up the printed book itself. The cover of the British edition, illustrated by Thomas Taylor, firmly established Harry's appearance (Bloomsbury also printed a serious-looking cover for adults featuring a photograph of a steam train so that adults could feel more comfortable reading a children's book in public). But Levine selected Mary GrandPré to illustrate the United States edition and added rich paper and decorative chapter illustrations to the Scholastic edition as well.

Meanwhile, since its debut in the United Kingdom in June 1997, sales of the novel were beginning to soar. "Reviews for the 80,000-word novel have been ecstatic," trumpeted the *Guardian*, "with the *Scotsman* [newspaper] lauding it as 'an unassailable stand for the power of fresh innovative story-telling in the face of formula horror and sickly romance.'"

In 1998, *Harry Potter and the Sorcerer's Stone* appeared in the United States. With the power of Scholastic's 80 million-member book club behind it, the brand new novelist

Did you know...

If you think the customs at Harry's boarding school are outlandish, British author Pico Iyer says they're not too far off the mark in his essay, "The Playing Fields of Hogwarts":

As a boy, I went for many years to the Dragon School in Oxford. The rooms in which we lived were called 'Leviathan' and 'Pterodactyl' and 'Ichthyosaurus'; the men who instructed us in dead languages were (through some arcane local custom) known always by their nicknames—'Guv' and 'Plum'and 'Inky' . . . The main languages we learned, from the ages of 7 to 14, were ones that had been out of use for 2,000 years or more, and Friday nights would find us bouncing up and down in our pajamas, reciting the principal parts of Greek irregular verbs. Every Sunday night, in our flowing black robes (we were known as 'tugs'), we would gather in a classroom dating from 1441 to sing hymns in Latin, and whenever we passed a 'beak'—i.e., a teacher—in the street, we were allowed to greet him only by raising one solemn finger silently into the air. . . . Here are all the rites I remember as vividly as lemon drops: the cryptic list of instructions that would appear through the mail, describing what we must—and mustn't—bring to school (the point of all the rules being not to make order so much as to enforce obedience); the trip to dusty old shops with creaky family names—New & Lingwood or Alden & Blackwell— where aged men would fit us out with the approved uniform and equipment, as they had done for our fathers and our fathers' fathers; the special school train that would be waiting in a London station to transport us to our cells.

saw her book climb the bestseller lists effortlessly. Two Hollywood studios expressed interest in a film version. In fact, media excitement on the overnight success of Harry Potter temporarily overwhelmed the young author. Worried that the next book in the series, *Harry Potter and the Chamber of Secrets* wouldn't be as good, she struggled with a case of writer's block and the pressure of the sequel's anticipation.

By now, Rowling already had the seven-book series clearly mapped out—in fact, she even had the ending to the final book written. But Bloomsbury had not contracted with her for more than one book. Nevertheless, she had been working on the entire series even as *Harry Potter and the Philosopher's Stone* made its modest debut with 500 copies. To get to work right away on sequels was a fortunate decision on her part, and a tremendous stroke of financial luck for her publishers, as it turned out.

Many authors of books for children and adolescents wait years before writing a sequel, during which time their readers outgrow the stories. A new "Ramona" book by Beverly Cleary was published in 1999; the first was published in 1952, the last in 1984. But Rowling kept most of her readers on the hook by being ready with a second title in the series. No sooner had *Harry Potter and the Sorcerer's Stone* achieved bestsellerdom in the United States than word circulated among Rowling fans that the second book was on its way.

In fact, some fans refused to wait. When *Harry Potter and the Chamber of Secrets* appeared in Britain in July 1998, thousands of young readers figured out how to order the Bloomsbury edition from Amazon.com's British site before it became available in the United States. Scholastic roared in protest, pointing out that only it had the legal right to sell the

A life-size replica of "Fluffy" the three-headed dog who guards the Sorcerer's Stone in the Harry Potter book stands behind a Tiger Electronics representative showing off some other Potter-related toys.

book in the United States. Amazon countered that the Internet was revolutionizing the nature of business, including book-selling. Apparently unable to stem the tide of Potter-mania, Scholastic responded by moving up the publication date of Rowling's second novel from September to June 1999.

Crowds in Chicago line up for a book signing by Rowling. The hysteria surrounding Rowling and Potter is rare for the book world, and seems more befitting of other kinds of celebrities.

    Harry Potter and the Chamber of Secrets opens with Harry finishing a particularly horrible summer at home with the Dursleys. He can't wait to return to Hogwarts to begin his second year. Banished to his bedroom by the Dursleys, he receives a visit from an elf named Dobby who warns him not return to school after all, for great danger awaits him there. But Ron Weasley and his brothers free Harry from his prison bedroom with their flying car. Despite Dobby's warnings, Harry returns to Hogwarts and stumbles right into the mystery of the Chamber of Secrets.

    On Halloween night, Harry, Ron and Hermione find a

message painted on a wall that reads, "The Chamber of Secrets has been opened. Enemies of the Heir, beware." The Chamber of Secrets contains a deadly monster. Sealed for fifty years, the last time the chamber *was* opened, someone died. "The heir" in the message refers to a descendant of one of the school's four founders, Salazar Slytherin, who had an affinity for the dark side of magic. Apparently, only Slytherin's heir would be able to open the Chamber of Secrets and use the monster within to cleanse the school from all "muggle-borns" and "halfbloods" whom he believed were unworthy to study magic. Now that the Chamber is open again, fear reigns at Hogwarts as students who don't come from "pureblood" wizarding families are found petrified. Harry and his friends must solve the mystery before the monster goes beyond merely petrifying its victims, and kills again. Inevitably, Lord Voldemort takes a hand in trying to defeat Harry and his friends.

By July 1999, just a month after the release of Rowling's second novel, there were 826,000 copies in print of *Harry Potter and the Sorcerer's Stone* and 915,000 of *Harry Potter and the Chamber of Secrets*. "At bedtime, at the beach, by the pool, in the back of the car," wrote the *New York Times*, "whole families are reading about the boarding school where the food is delicious and the equipment list includes a wand and a cauldron."

The magic of Harry Potter had become a phenomenon in publishing history.

Executives of the People's Literature Publishing House show the new Harry Potter book translated into Chinese in Beijing, further proof of Harry Potter's universal appeal.

6

A Phenomenon in Publishing

"I've been doing kids' books for 10 years, and I've never seen anything like this, kids coming in and saying give me something like this book."

— a bookseller quoted in the
New York Times, February 28, 2000

THERE'S A SAYING that "a rising tide floats all boats," meaning that a positive force acts on all things that it can affect, big or small. By the time news of Rowling's third book, *Harry Potter and the Prisoner of Azkaban*, had reached youngsters, librarians, booksellers, and the media, the "rising tide" of Harry Potter was beginning to be felt throughout the children's book publishing industry, too.

By coincidence, another series aimed at young readers had just peaked in popularity. Earlier in the 1990s, Scholastic's paperback series "Goosebumps" attracted a huge following among readers age 8-12, especially boys. With titles like *Chicken, Chicken; Haunted Mask; Phantom of the Auditorium; Beware of the Purple Peanut Butter;* and *Please Don't Feed the Vampire,* author and former children's magazine editor R. L. Stine turned out short, easy-to-read, scary tales with a humorous twist. Stine could hardly write them fast enough, even at 20 pages a day. At one point there were 57 books completed, another 42 planned, and 160 million in print. In 1997 about six million "Goosebumps" books sold a month in 15 different languages.

Did you know...

Harry Potter and The Goblet of Fire broke all publishing records by selling 372,775 copies on its first day.

But from a bookseller's point of view, R.L. Stine had a narrow impact on young people's reading interests. Said Clifford Wohl, a former children's bookseller, in an interview with the *New York Times*, "You couldn't get them off that dime. You couldn't say, 'Here's another scary book you might like.' No. They only wanted 'Goosebumps.' It was like a fence, and the boys were trapped within the series." Then, almost as quickly as "Goosebumps" had caught on, fans lost their taste for it. The ripple effect was that the children's paperback market dipped by almost 20 percent in the late 1990s. In 1999, the Association of American Publishers forecasted gloom for children's book sales. But actually, the association underestimated the percentage growth in children's hard-cover sales by more than half. According to an association member who had helped develop the prediction, no one in bookselling had foreseen the arrival of Harry Potter.

The beauty of Harry Potter was that the quality of the writing and the story sent fans hurrying to find similar books. "I've been doing kids' books for 10 years, and I've never seen anything like this, kids coming in and saying give me some-thing like this book," remarked a children's buyer for the Joseph-Beth Booksellers chain based in Cincinnati, Ohio. Major newspapers began referring to the "halo effect" of Harry Potter encouraging young readers to try books like Brian Jacques' *Redwall* series, for example, as well as older titles in children's fantasy literature. In 1999, Harry Potter accounted for much of the growth in children's literature—an increase in paperback sales of 24 percent to $660 million, and an increase in hardback sales of 11 percent to $1.6 million.

The boy with glasses and a broomstick had become a phenomenon in publishing. Confident that Rowling's appeal would stay strong, Scholastic debuted her third book, *Harry Potter and the Prisoner of Azkaban*, with first-print runs of 900,000 in the United States, while Bloomsbury printed 275,000 in Britain and the rest of the United Kingdom in markets like Canada and Australia.

At the beginning of *Harry Potter and the Prisoner of Azkaban*, Harry has spent yet another miserable summer at home with the Dursleys and can't wait to get back to school at Hogwarts. He's especially looking forward to the third-year privilege of visiting the all-magical village of Hogsmeade near the school. The only problem is that he must get Uncle Vernon to sign his permission slip to do so. He strikes a bargain with his uncle, which backfires when Harry angrily but accidentally "inflates" Aunt Marge. At risk now of being

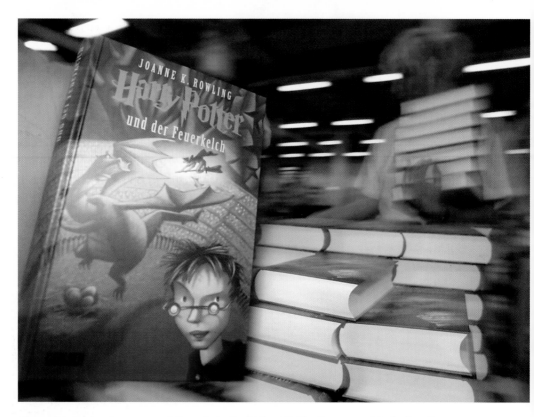

Harry Potter books prepared for sale in Bad Hersfeld in Germany. Undoubtedly the busiest places before the sale date of Harry Potter books are the warehouses that must ensure that all the bookstores have enough stock to meet demand.

punished by the Ministry of Magic for the improper use of magic by an underage wizard, Harry tries to run away. Fortunately, he is picked up by a magical bus and delivered to Diagon Alley, where he is able to meet his Hogwarts friends and purchase his school supplies for the upcoming year.

Instead of being punished by the Ministry of Magic, Harry discovers that he is actually being protected. The murderous and dreadful Sirius Black has escaped from Azkaban, the wizard prison, and Harry is believed to be his next victim. Soon, Black gains access into Hogwarts, threatening Harry's welfare even in his own dormitory. The mystery for Harry, Ron and Hermione now involves figuring out Sirius Black's original crime, whether he is connected to Harry's parents and their deaths, and if Black is the traitor who informed on Harry's parents to Voldemort. In working out this puzzle, Harry finds both his father's best friends and his own godfather. Even though Harry, Ron and Hermione do find the traitor, he escapes in the end, leaving both Voldemort and one of his henchmen to haunt Harry in the next volume.

When *Harry Potter and the Prisoner of Azkaban* was

Did you know...

For the audiobook version of *Harry Potter and the Goblet of Fire*, British actor and songwriter Jim Dale created 125 speaking voices. Mr. Dale, 64, has acted on stage and films, been a disc jockey, a pop music and television star in Britain.

Sitting in the recording booth, Mr. Dale told the *New York Times*, "I visualized the reactions of children listening." He has five grandchildren. "Stunned silence here! So hold the break two, three, four . . . This line is worth a giggle, it deserves more than a laugh, pause, two, three, so their shouts don't drown the next line. That's what more than 40 years of being on stage teaches you."

He said the most difficult aspect of narrating was not keeping all those voices straight, but sitting absolutely still, because the microphones could pick up the rustle of cloth as he crossed his pants legs!

released in September of 1999, all three titles captured the first, second, and third slots on the *New York Times* Bestseller List, remaining there for months afterwards. By then, Rowling also had won the prestigious British Smarties Book Prize three years in a row, becoming the first author to do so. She requested that future Harry Potter titles not be considered for the award to give other authors a better chance. In 2000, *Forbes* magazine named Rowling to its annual Celebrity 100 list as the 24th-highest celebrity earner in the world, having earned $40 million in 1999. Worldwide sales of the first three Harry Potter books reached 30 million in 35 languages.

Until now, Rowling had managed to avoid interviews, deciding "that I would give interviews—when I had something to say." But with media curiosity and even some controversy swirling now around the author and her books, she began agreeing to interviews after the publication of *Harry Potter and the Prisoner of Azkaban.* The author turned out to be assertive, opinionated, and astute—not at all like the romantic image painted of her by the press. In fact, she resented being described over and over as a "'penniless single mother,'" as she put it, who made good. She pointed out that she had a college education. Despite that "There is the sense of 'Oooh, what a miracle!' as if it's superhuman for single parents to achieve anything. But then I've occasionally detected a 'Well, they can do it if they have to', which is equally unfair," she said.

Likewise, in a radio interview with the British Broadcasting System (BBC), she addressed head-on several issues about the Harry Potter books. First, there was a growing background rumble by some critics who argued that the topics in her books—evil, death, and murder, for instance—were unsuitable for small children. She admitted that might be true, saying "I do think that, on occasion, the material is not suitable for six-year-olds. But you can't stop them reading it . . . . so I wouldn't say 'Don't read them [the books] to a six-year-old,' just be aware some of it does get uncomfortable." She added that the Harry Potter books deal with evil, and how evil it is to take a human life. "If you are going to write about those kinds of things," she said, "you have a moral obligation to show what that involves, not to prettify it or to minimize it."

She also denied that she had hit on a formula for writing bestselling children's books, or that she knew what children wanted. "I sat down to write something I knew I would enjoy reading. I do not try to analyze it and I don't write to a formula. I always find it quite patronizing—'What do children want?' —as if they are a separate species. I do not write with an imaginary focus group of eight-year-olds in mind."

And finally, she voiced her unhappiness with newfound celebrity and the invasion of privacy that accompanies it. "When people start searching through your bins [garbage cans] it is horrible. It feels like such an invasion. I am not a politician, I am not an entertainer and I never expected this much interest in my life."

With so much attention suddenly forced upon her, Rowling understandably felt considerable pressure as she worked on the fourth book in the series, *Harry Potter and the Goblet of Fire*. It would have to be the cornerstone book of the series, after all—the one that provided enough energy and new plot developments to propel the series forward for three more books. If the series flagged in the middle, disappointed readers might abandon Harry Potter by the millions.

She put in ten-hour days on the manuscript. With the deadline closing in—already editors at Scholastic and Bloomsbury were strategizing how to build up excitement for the book—Rowling saw that the story was running much, much longer than she expected. Then disaster struck as she discovered that something was wrong with the plot. Midway through the novel, she realized she hadn't set up events to reach the conclusion she wanted. It was like building a house and then discovering its size is bigger than the foundation. She had no choice but to start over.

She finally submitted the finished manuscript to Bloomsbury. The Scholastic edition ran a whopping 734

Did you know...

The full name of the movie setting in England for Hogwarts school is Gloucester Cathedral: the Cathedral Church of St. Peter and the Holy and Indivisible Trinity. King Henry VIII established the cathedral in 1541.

Some Britons objected to using a sacred place as a location for a movie about magic, however. The Dean of Gloucester Cathedral, Nicholas Bury, made public his reply on a web site for visitors:

"I regard the books as most wholesome fantasy stories for children, which like all good children's novels, tackle some important issues for children in an imaginative, thoughtful and often very amusing way. The hero discovers his identity, the importance of relationships with his peers, that lies and deceit are corrosive and love conquers evil and so on. It is, I believe, far-fetched to think that anyone could be hurt by such good stories."

pages. On July 8, 2000 *Harry Potter and the Goblet of Fire* arrived in bookstores amid an unprecedented amount of publicity for a children's book, or perhaps any book. In fact, British author Anthony Holden thought the hoopla was ridiculous and undeserved. In an opinion piece appearing in *The Observer* in London, he complained, "Haven't Bloomsbury sold enough copies of J.K. Rowling's three volumes so far without resorting to advance hype worthy of a Wonderbra." He called the books "Disney cartoons written in words, no more." A week after his attack, the *Observer* published two pages of responses, mostly from young readers, defending Rowling and accusing Holden of being jealous.

Then an unsettling rumor began to circulate, after nearly 3 million copies of the new book were in the eager hands of readers. There was a mistake, the rumor went—a key mistake in the order in which Voldemort had killed people. During the battle between Voldemort and Harry in the climatic confrontation near the end of the fourth book, Harry forces the ghosts of all those whom Voldemort has killed with his wand to eject themselves momentarily into the living world. They emerge in the reverse of the order in which they were killed. First comes Cedric, the popular Hogwarts Quidditch player, who was most recently killed by Voldemort, then the groundskeeper of the Riddle Estate, then "missing" witch Bertha Jorkins, followed by Harry's parents.

But here's where there seems to be a mistake—Harry's father comes out first, followed by his mother. In the first book, Rowling makes clear that Harry's father died first, in an attempt to protect his wife and child, and that only after his failure was Harry's mother killed. So if the ghosts of Voldemort's victims appear in reverse order, shouldn't his mother come out first and then his father? So far, the discrepancy remains a mystery. But Rowling is a careful plotter, so it's hard to believe the surprise is just an oversight on her part.

In *Harry Potter and the Goblet of Fire*, the first 75 pages mainly review important events in the first three books. Nearly 1,000 printed pages of story have gone before this volume, so it's as though Rowling wants to make certain her readers are prepared for her longest title yet. But the new information readers discover is that Voldemort is on the move again. Meanwhile, Harry escapes his summer "imprisonment" at the Dursleys' to attend the Quidditch World Cup with the Weasley family and Hermione. Thousands of international witches and wizards have gathered at the Cup. But chaos erupts when the "Dark Mark"—Voldemort's sign—appears in the sky.

Returning to Hogwarts for his fourth year, Harry finds only a few of his classmates are concerned about the Dark Mark. Everyone is more interested in news of the Triwizard Tournament, a contest between the wizard champions of Hogwarts, Durmstrang, and Beauxbaton, the three largest schools of magic. Harry is still too young to be chosen as Hogwarts' official school champion, but someone finds a way to enter him in the contest anyway—perhaps as a compliment, or maybe as a trick. Once chosen, Harry *must* participate. It soon clear that whoever entered his name did so intending him harm.

During the year-long competition, champions complete three magical tasks, hoping to win honor for their school and a monetary prize for themselves. There's a connection between Dark Mark seen in the sky and the Triwizard Tournament, however. Also, something is fishy about the new professor for Defense Against the Dark Arts. Hermione finds her own cause apart from Harry's this time, in the form of liberating the house elves from "slavery." But everyone close to Harry gets fed up with muckraking journalist

Rita Skeeter, who seems determined to ruin his life.

Then, no sooner has the Triwizard tournament ended with a twist and the victory celebration is underway than Harry is drawn into another battle with Voldemort. Rowling delivers on her promise that a well-liked character will die. Harry escapes with his life, but the end of this story spells more-than-usual concern for the future, because Voldemort has regained his body, which he had lost when he tried to kill infant Harry. As the book ends, Professor Dumbledore entreats the international wizarding community to stand united against the dark side.

Said film and book critic Janet Maslin of the *New York Times*, "As the midpoint in a projected seven-book series, *Goblet of Fire* is exactly the big, clever, vibrant, tremendously assured installment that gives shape and direction to the whole undertaking and still somehow preserves the material's enchanting innocence."

Death figures importantly in the fourth book, but Rowling told the *New York Times* it wasn't the hardest issue for her to handle. The series after all began with the death of Harry's parents. Instead, she said developing Rita Skeeter, the nosy journalist with little respect for the truth or people's privacy was the most difficult. "I knew people would assume that this was my response to what's happened to me," she said, referring to how a few journalists had hounded her or distorted the facts of her life. But she decided to go ahead with the character and risk a possible backlash from the media.

Readers were unconcerned with what the media might think. By August 2000, *Harry Potter and the Goblet of Fire* joined Rowling's three other titles on the New York Times Bestseller List. With her books dominating the 68-year-old list, editors at the *New York Times* decided it was time for a change and created a bestseller list specifically for children's books. On the new list, Harry Potter took the top four spots, followed by 11 other children's and young adult titles. Publishers were divided on whether or not a children's book list was a good idea.

"It's been a long time coming," remarked Joanna Cotler, publisher of Joanna Cotler Books at HarperCollins Children's, "and I'm thrilled that Harry Potter is what finally pushed them into it. I've always looked at the *New York Times*' bestseller list as wonderful free advertising. Now children's books get it, too." Barbara Marcus, president of the Scholastic Children's Book Group, J.K. Rowling's American publisher, disagreed. To her, the success of Harry Potter annoyed other publishers, and so the *New York Times* banished children's

Did you know...

Steven Spielberg turned down directing the film version of Harry Potter when Rowling refused to go along with his wish to put Hogwarts in the United States and Haley Joel Osment in the part of Harry. Chris Columbus eventually landed the directorship of Harry Potter. But who else might have directed the film? Other directors mentioned by the press as possible candidates included Rob Reiner ("Sleepless in Seattle"), Alan Parker ("Angela's Ashes") and Guillermo del Toro ("Mimic"), but the finalist who seems to appeal most to Potter buffs was Terry Gilliam ("Time Bandits," "Twelve Monkeys"). "Sixth Sense" director M. Night Shyamalan and Tim Burton ("Beetlejuice") were other favorites.

books to their own list. "The *Times* became a spoiler of it all. I always believed that bestseller lists are just that, and they should be recording and *reporting* the bestselling books in the country," Marcus told Salon.com.

Rowling tries to stay away from the fray of controversy and fame created by Harry Potter as much as possible. To this day, she treasures being able to walk down a street in Edinburgh unnoticed. About her private life she said, "It's not particularly interesting—seeing friends, working, raising a daughter—the most important thing in my life, Harry included."

But being famous creates avoidable challenges, too. When Jessica was still only five or six, for instance, classmates quizzed her relentlessly about Harry Potter, refusing to believe her mother had not read her the books (which she really hadn't done). Rowling told school authorities Jessica needed to be left alone. But then when she discovered Jessica was asking other children about Harry Potter, she decided it was time to read her the books.

One more unanticipated dilemma of being the most popular children's author in the world has to with money. Rowling is one of the richest women in Britain, and she says the extent of her sudden wealth makes her somewhat uncomfortable.

"Yes, I'm riddled with guilt," Rowling admits about her wealth. "It's a very weird situation. Then again, there is a solution. You can give it away. You can't sit there and say, 'Ah, it's tragic, I've got a lot of money', because nobody's stopping you spreading it about a bit." So she contributes to the work of the Multiple Sclerosis Society of Scotland in memory of her mother. In addition, the former jobless parent of an infant daughter is also the ambassador for the National Council For One Parent Families in Britain.

A midnight sale in New York for Harry Potter and the Goblet of Fire. *Alexandra Korves, age 9, was the first person to purchase the book at the Books of Wonder store at 12:01 a.m.*

7

What Critics Say About the Books

"Rowling says she had no wish at all to upset children but she does want to write the story her way. 'I have good reason for doing it. There are certain things I want to explore and if it's the last thing I do, I will not be knocked off course.'"

—*USA Today*, July 9, 2000

WHEN ANYTHING ARTISTIC—A television program, a movie, a CD of songs, a fashion craze, or a book, for example—becomes popular, it invites analysis. People naturally want to identify why something is popular because it might shed light on what matters to us as human beings. Classic love songs are said to capture certain feelings of love, for example. Great movies with serious themes are often praised for dramatizing emotional conflicts in people's lives.

Likewise, the Harry Potter series has not escaped analysis. How could they when millions of children on several continents have read them, and will continue to read them? Books that have influenced so directly the reading tastes of young people and appeal to them so strongly are certain to be analyzed on different levels.

The first level the Harry Potter books are judged on is literary, because they are stories after all. And as a story-teller, Rowling has been called "a fine stylist and a clever fantasist," even if she has always maintained, "I just write what I wanted to write. I write what amuses me. It's totally for myself. I never in my wildest dreams expected this popularity." An editor of *The Times Literary Supplement* in London expressed the opinion of many critics that, as engaging stories with positive themes, the Rowling's books deserved to be liked. "It takes an extremely curmudgeonly attitude to despise these books," he wrote.

On the other hand, other critics applying stricter standards for judging literature have not been as complimentary. In a *Wall Street Journal* article, Harold Bloom, Sterling Professor of Humanities at Yale University said of Rowling's writing, "Her prose style, heavy on clichés, makes no demands upon her readers." Robert McCrum, the literary editor of *The Observer*, wrote a review that otherwise praised Rowling as a storyteller, but added, "Her work . . . has the reader by the throat from page to page, but her prose is as flat (and as English) as old beer."

In Rowling's defense, other reviewers have argued that because adults enjoy her books does not mean they should be measured against writing aimed at adults. After all, the Harry Potter books are written for children. Nationally syndicated columnist William Safire went further and scolded adults for "buying these books ostensibly to read to kids, but actually to read for themselves . . . . this is not just dumbing down; it is growing down. The purpose of reading, once you get the hang of it, is not merely to follow the action of a plot, but to learn about characters, explore different ideas and enter other minds."

Even when compared with other books for children, Harry sometimes comes in second. After the ballots were counted for awarding Britain's Carnegie Medal, Britain's most prestigious award for children's books, Annie Everall, the head of the 12-member judging panel, announced the panels' conclusions just before *Goblet of Fire* was published. She said that the opinion of the panel was that Harry was "more one-dimensional" than rivals for the prize. As McCrum put it in *The Observer*, "[Harry] is not a boy of depth or subtlety."

Did you know...

The American Library Association maintains a list of the 100 most frequently challenged books. The top three reasons, in order, for challenges to books and other reading material are that the text is considered "sexually explicit," or that it contains "offensive language," or that it is "unsuited to the age group." On the list of 100 most frequently challenged books between 1990-2000, the Harry Potter series ranks seventh.

Debates like these over the literary merits of Harry Potter haven't kept the books out of any child's hands, of course. Whether or not critics agree on Rowling's abilities as a novelist, her millions of young readers serve as proof that she succeeds the world over as a much-loved storyteller. A far more serious challenge to the Harry Potter books has come from another set of critics who object to what the books rely on—the concept of magic.

Did you know...

American author Nancy K. Stouffer completed *The Legend of Rah and the Muggles* in 1984. In 2000, she sued Scholastic, claiming that Rowling's book infringed on her copyright. She cited, as one example, her use of the word "muggles." The word "muggles," she says, comes from her son's baby-talk word for cheeks—muggles. Rowling says her Muggles came from a British word for fool.

Actually, the word is older than both writers, according to the *Washington Post*. "The *Oxford English Dictionary* traces muggles back to the 13th century, when muggles meant 'tails.' By the 20th century, the word had come to mean marijuana, and in the 1920s a pot smoker was called a muggle-head. In the 1930s Louis Armstrong had a song called 'Muggles.' And in 1960 Carol Kendall's novel *The Gammage Cup*, written for young people featured a character named Muggles. It was a Newbery Award honor book."

No well-known group or organization has stepped forward and mounted a campaign against the Harry Potter books, but objections tend to follow a pattern. Young adult novelist Judy Blume said in the *New York Times,* "With Harry Potter, the perceived danger is fantasy. After all, Harry and his classmates attend the celebrated Hogwarts School of Witchcraft and Wizardry. According to certain adults, these stories teach witchcraft, sorcery and satanism." The conservative Christian magazine *Focus on the Family* is specific: "the danger of Rowling's books is the fact that, though witches and wizards aren't portrayed *realistically,* they (at least the 'good' ones) are portrayed *positively*." The magazine feared "desensitization to witchcraft," meaning that young people may be encouraged to accept it as normal.

It's worth noting, though, that self-proclaimed witches have not rushed to embrace the Harry Potter books, either. "It really doesn't have anything to do with us," said a Wiccan priest who lives in Plymouth, England. "I've read these books, since I wanted to see what was in them before I gave them to my kids, and I must say that these books no more promote witchcraft than *Anne of Green Gables* promotes moving to Nova Scotia."

Asked whether an author should have a moral sense of responsibility when it comes to children, Rowling has said that she does not write thinking about "here's the moral lessons we are going to teach our children. None of that ever enters my head. I write what I want to write." In any case, she has said the objections to magic and wizardy in her work miss the point anyway. "The book is really about the power of the imagination. What Harry is learning to do is to develop his full potential. Wizardry is just the analogy I use."

And developing one's potential may be the most important

Amazon.com.uk employees in the Milton Keyes, London distribution center prepare 65,000 copies of Harry Potter and the Goblet of Fire, *the biggest seller in the history of online book sales, according to Amazon's figures.*

reason why the Potter books are so popular— because they reassure and encourage. All young people wonder at some time or another whether they are special in some way. At the very beginning of *Harry Potter and the Sorcerer's Stone,* Harry too has a moment of doubt about whether he has what it takes to become a wizard.

Scholastic vice president Arthur A. Levine, who purchased

the rights to publish Harry Potter in the United States for the highest amount ever bid for a foreign children's book, knew why the story appealed to him. "The thing I loved the most about reading Harry Potter," said Levine, "is the idea of growing up unappreciated, feeling outcast and then this great satisfaction of being discovered. That is the fantasy of every person who grows up feeling marginalized in any way."

New York Times film critic A.O. Scott offered similar personal reasons. "You feel, somehow, that they [the books] have always been there, waiting for you to discover. You also feel, in spite of being one of several million crazed fans, that they were written for you alone, a wizard stranded in an uncomprehending Muggle world, waiting for someone to recognize that what everyone else calls your abnormalities are really powers."

Did you know...

According to the Boarding Education Alliance in Britain, the Harry Potter books have helped sell the notion of boarding to a new generation of parents and students. Did Rowling ever want to go to boarding school? No, she says, the first time she met anyone who'd been to boarding school was at university. "I thought it sounded horrible. Not because I was so attached to home—I couldn't wait to leave home—just that the culture was not one I'd enjoy. It staggers me to meet people who want to send their kids away."

Rowling with one of the winners of the essay contest "How the Harry Potter Books Changed My Life" in New York. Many credit Rowling with making reading fun for young children as well as rejuvenating children's book sales across the board.

8

Harry's Place in Children's Literature

"Then she can't get back," shouted Digory. "And it's exactly the same as if you'd murdered her!'

'She can get back,' said Uncle Andrew, 'if someone else will go after her, wearing a yellow ring himself and taking two green rings, one to bring himself back and one to bring her back.'

And now of course Digory saw the trap in which he was caught . . ."

—C.S. Lewis, *The Magician's Nephew*
in *The Chronicles of Narnia*

IN C.S. LEWIS' *The Chronicles of Narnia* (1956) children move back and forth between reality and fantastic worlds using magic. They are up to the task of fighting evil wherever they find it, in this world or another one. A few adults or authority figures can be trusted around magic, but most are too unimaginative, mean, or incompetent to be dependable— a repeated theme in young people's fantasy literature. Other well-known books in this vein include Lewis Carroll's *Alice in Wonderland* (1865), L. Frank Baum's *The Wizard of Oz*, and Ursula K. Le Guin's *The Wizard of Earthsea* (1968).

And then there's Harry Potter. Where do Rowling's books fit in the long line of fantasy books written for young people? Are they something new, or do they draw on themes, conflicts, and settings that have fascinated young readers for a long time?

To begin with, Rowling's use of magic continues a tradition that is as old as beanstalks, witches, enchanted forests, and potions. From the very beginning of *Harry Potter and the Sorcerer's Stone*, readers plunge into a reality outside the normal one. In the first chapter, sorcerers Dumbledore and Professor McGonagall meet on a suburban street and discuss amazing events. A deadly battle has taken place between wizards, and an exceptional child named Harry has somehow survived! Not many pages later, the humdrum world of Privet Drive is joyously left behind as Harry and Rowling's readers depart for the world of magic from Platform 9 3/4 at King's Cross Station.

Rowling also develops her books using another long-standing tradition in young people's literature: settings where young characters live among their peers. In Harry's case, it's Hogwarts School of Witchcraft and Wizardry. More than a century ago, Rudyard Kipling made popular a school setting for the adventures of boys outwitting their teachers in *Stalky & Co.*, which became a model for count-less other authors. Schools make excellent stages for drama. In Robert Cormier's *The Chocolate War* (1974) the boring adult world barely exists beyond the walls of Trinity. Inside the school, wrong clashes with right practically every day.

And because Rowling is writing for young readers, the challenges of relying on oneself and growing up are central to her books, which is at the heart of all first-rate literature for young people. It would be hard to find a Newbery

Did you know...

Will Harry Potter become a classic of children's literature? According to Alan Cowell in his New York Times article, "The Subtlety of Hogwarts? Give a Wizard a Break!" most critics speak highly of Rowling's books, but there are also those who don't think it will become a classic:

"Some skeptics, like Jeff Baker, a book critic for *The Portland Oregonian*, are prepared to concede that the books are 'well written and extremely imaginative' but echo the view that Harry Potter is not yet assured of a place in the annals of great children's literature. 'J. K. Rowling is a fine stylist and a clever fantasist,' he wrote, 'but she is no J. R. R. Tolkien. *The Hobbit* and *The Lord of the Rings* are more exciting and, frankly, more beautiful than the Potter series, and C. S. Lewis's amazing *The Chronicles of Narnia* series, which Rowling often cites as an influence, is more poetic and fully formed.'"

award-winner for children's literature, for instance, such as Richard Peck's *A Year Down Yonder* (2001) or Chistopher Paul Curtis's *Bud, Not Buddy* (2000) that didn't have exploring growing up at its core.

But what makes the plots of Rowling's books so riveting to young readers may have to do with the most powerful tradition in children's literature of all: the fairytale education of the hero. Fairytale heroes such as "Cinderella," "The Ugly Duckling," "Hansel and Gretel" and "Little Red Riding Hood" (and their similar counterparts in other cultures) follow much the same path. First, they start off in an ordinary world. But quickly, they move into an enchanted world. Hansel and Gretel get lost in a forest and find a gingerbread house belonging to a witch. Little Red Riding Hood also enters a forest where a clever wolf takes advantage of her trusting nature. But eventually, each fairytale hero must face trials of courage, loyalty, or ingenuity and overcome his or her weaknesses—sometimes with help from others—in order to overcome adversity.

But fairytales are short in length. That's because they were oral tales, told to listeners in various versions, long before they were collected by writers such as the Brothers Grimm and Hans Christian Andersen. In the late nineteenth and early twentieth centuries, longer fantasy stories for young people began appearing, such as *Alice in Wonderland* and J. M. Barrie's tremendously popular play *Peter Pan* (1904). Like fairytales, these used enchantment as a means to move the story along. But the characters in the story didn't really follow the hero's path yet. Alice is still the same Alice, even after she falls down the rabbit hole. An exception is *Pinocchio* (1892) by Carlo Collodi, who finds the qualities within himself, step-by-step, to become a real boy. *Pinocchio* has enchantment, even a fairy that guides him—essentially a hero's tale.

From the late 1930s on, authors of some of the great English fantasies for young people combined both fairytales and the hero's progress into book-length fantasies for young people. In J.R.R. Tolkien's novel *The Hobbit* (1937), shy Bilbo Baggins finds himself called upon to do great deeds in a fantasy world, and learn to be heroic in the process. In T.H. White's *The Sword in the Stone* (1939), bumbling Wart is

Did you know...

If you like the Harry Potter books, here are other titles you may enjoy:

The Chronicles of Prydain (series) by Lloyd Alexander
A young pigkeeper has adventures far above his place in society: battling the Horned King, destroying the Black Cauldron, and rescuing the Princess Eilonwy.

The Lost Years of Merlin by T.A. Baron
A young boy who has no identity or memory of his past washes ashore on the coast of Wales and finds his true name after a series of fantastic adventures. Sequel: **The Seven Songs of Merlin**

The Dark Secret of Weatherend by John Bellairs
Fourteen-year-old Anthony Mundy and the town librarian try to prevent an evil wizard from turning the world into an icy wasteland.

The Witches by Roald Dahl
A boy and his grandmother thwart the plans of England's witches to turn all children into mice.

So You Want to Be a Wizard by Diane Duane
Thirteen-year-old Nita finds the help she needs in a library book on wizardry and is guided into another dimension where she earns her degree in wizardry. Sequels: **Deep Wizardry; High Wizardry; A Wizard Abroad**

The Neverending Story by Michael Ende
Bastian travels through the aptly named realm of Fantastica to complete a noble quest.

Redwall by Brian Jacques
When life at ancient Redwall Abbey is shattered by the evil rat Cluny, Matthias determines to find the legendary sword of Martin the Warrior, which will help Redwall's inhabitants destroy the enemy. Sequels: **Mossflower; Mattimeo; Mariel of Redwall; and others**

The Dark Lord of Derkholm by Diana Wynne Jones
An unconventional wizard and his magical family become involved in a plan to stop the devastating tours of their world arranged by tyrannical Mr. Chesney.

The Lives of Christopher Chant
Christopher discovers that his dreams are so realistic that he can actually visit other worlds and bring things back from them for his beloved, yet mysterious, uncle. Also: **Magicians of Caprona; Charmed Life; Witch Week**

Phantom Tollbooth by Norton Juster
Finding a car and a tollbooth in his bedroom, Milo drives off to rescue the lost princesses aided by the Spelling Bee and a watchdog named Tock.

A Wizard of Earthsea by Ursula K. Le Guin
A boy grows to manhood while attempting to subdue the evil he unleashed on the world as an apprentice to the Master Wizard.

Wrinkle in Time by Madeline L'Engle
When an atomic physicist disappears on a secret mission, his son and daughter and their friend search for him, going on an interplanetary journey through time and space. Sequels: **Wind in the Door; a Swiftly Tilting Planet**

Five Children and It by E. Nesbit
While digging in a sandpit, the children discover a Psammead—a creature with mysterious powers who leads the children into adventure and excitement. Sequels: **The Phoenix and the Carpet; The Story of the Amulet**

The Golden Compass by Philip Pullman
Accompanied by her animal-like daemon, Lyra tries to prevent her best friend and other kidnapped children from being the subject of experiments. Sequel: **The Subtle Knife**

The Hobbit by J.R.R. Tolkein
Bilbo Baggins, a respectable, well-to-do hobbit, lives comfortably in his hobbit-hole until the day the wandering wizard Gandalf chooses him to share in an adventure from which he may never return.

The Sword in the Stone by T.H. White
Merlin the Sorcerer teaches young King Arthur about magic and history. Also: **The Once and Future King**

Passager: The Young Merlin Trilogy, Book One by Jane Yolen
A foundling rediscovers his identity through the help of the falconer who adopts him. Sequels: **Hobby; Merlin**

Wizard's Hall
A young apprentice wizard saves the wizard's training hall by trusting and believing in himself.

taught by trial-and-error how to act and think like a hero by Merlyn the wizard.

It's in this category of writing—the fairytale-fantasy of a hero's journey—where Harry Potter resides. Moreover, young readers fall deeply under Rowling's spell because the age-old elements of enchantment, dark forces, cruel relatives, and a noble main character that make fairytales so appealing are present in the Harry Potter books.

One of the first things we learn about Harry is that the Dursleys are not his real parents, for instance. Instead, he is being raised by wicked stepparents. Actually, the Durselys aren't wicked so much as insensitive and stupid. They refuse to recognize any other world except their ordinary one, or to acknowledge that Harry is special. Many fairytale characters live like Cinderella in cruel families who fail to appreciate them. This strikes a chord with many children who believe that the parents they live with are not their real parents.

There is also a grand secret—another key element in fairytales—about Harry's family. His parents were sorcerers, and now, willing or not, he must live-up to his birthright. Almost the same secret drives all the Star Wars movies. Luke Skywalker believes he is just a farmer living with his aunt and uncle. Little does he know a mighty force for evil is headed his way. He has warrior blood in him and must heed the call to duty and adventure. Perhaps Harry will find out more about his birth too as Rowling completes her novels.

Unfortunately for Harry, he seems unfit for the job he's called upon to do— a big handicap shared by most fairytale heroes. He is meek, skinny, and wears glasses. He's picked on by his spoiled step-brother Dudley, the way Cinderella is ridiculed by her spoiled step-sisters. Harry seems powerless. Many children also feel this way themselves at times. Things don't improve much for him when he arrives at Hogwarts,

Rowling with Neil Murray at the film premiere of Harry Potter and the Philosopher's Stone *in London. The two married on December 26, 2001 in a private ceremony after an earlier attempt to marry in July was aborted after the press learned about it.*

either. Even though he belongs at Hogwarts because he's the son of famous and admired sorcerers, other students all seem to know more than he does. Worse, a bully hounds him, and a teacher takes a very unfair dislike to him. Is there any hope for Harry?

Yes there is, because in fairytales, heroes who face up to life's challenges are rewarded in the end. The child psychologist Bruno Bettelheim, in his acclaimed book on fairytales *The Uses of Enchantment*, points out that fairytales teach "that a struggle against severe difficulties in life is unavoidable, is an intrinsic part of human existence—but that if one does not shy away, but steadfastly meets unexpected and often unjust hardships, one masters all obstacles and at the end emerges victorious."

Perhaps Harry too will emerge victorious as he struggles to gain mastery over himself, over his powers, and one day even over his enemy, Lord Voldemort. That would be a fairytale ending.

1965 *July 31:* Joanne Kathleen Rowling is born at Chipping Sodbury General Hospital in Gloucestershire, England.

1971 Writes her first story, about a rabbit who gets the measles. The family moves from Yate to Winterbourne, near Bristol. She and her younger sister, Di, play with an adventurous brother and sister whose last name is Potter.

1974 Rowling family moves to Tutshill, near Chepstow in Wales, on the edge of the Forest of Dean. Begins collecting novels by her favorite children's authors.

1976 Enrolls at Wyedean Comprehensive. Nearby Wyedean School has Houses named Armstrong, Bannister, Chichester and Hillary. Best friend Sean Harris provides the model for Ron Weasley.

1980 Rowling's mother is diagnosed with multiple sclerosis.

1982 Becomes Head Girl, or lead pupil, at Wyedean Comprehensive.

1983 Enrolls at University of Exeter, studying French and classics.

1985 Spends one year in Paris as teaching assistant as part of degree.

1987 Graduates from Exeter, then works briefly as a research assistant for Amnesty International. Writes during lunch hours in pubs and cafes.

1988 Employed as a secretary in Manchester, but hates the work.

1990 During a long train ride from Manchester to London, suddenly imagines a boy who can do anything, but doesn't realize it. Idea for the setting— a school of witchcraft— occurs to her, too.

Mother dies at age 45 from multiple sclerosis.

1991 Takes a position teaching English as a foreign language in Oporto, Portugal. Writes ten different first chapters for *Harry Potter and the Philosopher's Stone.*

1992 Marries Portuguese television journalist.

1993 Gives birth to a daughter, Jessica.

Christmas: Divorces; returns to Britain with her daughter and settles in Edinburgh, Scotland to be near her sister.

1994 Struggles to make ends meet as a single parent who can't find a job that pays well enough to provide daycare for her daughter. Continues to work on Harry Potter whenever she can during the day, and at night.

1995 Sends finished manuscript to two agents and one publisher.

1996 Works as French teacher while waiting to hear about her manuscript.

1997 *February:* Scottish Arts Council gives her a large grant to continue writing. Finishes the second book in the series.

June: Harry Potter and the Philosopher's Stone published in Britain.

September: Scholastic purchases U.S. rights to *Harry Potter and the Philosopher's Stone.*

1998 *July: Harry Potter and the Chamber of Secrets* published in Britain.

1999 *July: Harry Potter and the Prisoner of Azkaban* published in Britain, becoming the No. 1 bestseller. Harry Potter books are also the top three titles on the New York Times fiction bestseller list.

2000 Makes Forbes magazine's annual Celebrity 100 list as the 24th-highest celebrity earner in the world.

March: Worldwide sales of Harry Potter books reach 30 million in 35 languages.

July: Harry Potter and the Goblet of Fire published both in Britain and the United States at the same time.

2001 *November:* Warner Brother's releases the movie, "Harry Potter."

1997　*Harry Potter and the Philosopher's Stone*
1998　*Harry Potter and the Chamber of Secrets*
1999　*Harry Potter and the Prisoner of Azkaban*
2000　*Harry Potter and the Goblet of Fire*

1998 *Harry Potter and the Philosopher's Stone*

1999 *Harry Potter and the Chamber of Secrets*

Harry Potter and the Prisoner of Azkaban

2000 *Harry Potter and the Goblet of Fire*

Harry Potter and the Sorcerer's Stone - Collector's Edition

2001 Harry Potter Schoolbooks: "Magical Beasts and Where to Find Them" and "Quidditch through the Ages" (Benefit for the Comic Relief Foundation)

2002 *Harry Potter and the Order of the Phoenix*

HARRY POTTER

Harry Potter, the hero of the series, is a boy with black hair, green eyes framed by a pair of glasses, and a lightening-shaped scar on his forehead. His parents were killed during a battle of magic between themselves and the evil wizard Lord Voldemort. Harry is modest, yet loyal, courageous, and morally upright. His years at Hogwarts learning to become a wizard form the overall framework of the books.

RONALD WEASLEY

Ron is Harry's best friend—tall with red hair and freckles—the sixth of seven children in his family. His brothers all did very well at Hogwarts, which casts a kind of shadow over Ron's hard-won accomplishments. He is faithful and always ready for adventure, even if he is a little clumsy.

HERMIONE GRANGER

Hermione, friend of both Ron and Harry, is at the top of her class, even though her family are Muggles. She is clever and first-rate at solving problems, yet sympathetic too. By her toughness and fairness, she inspires others.

DRACO MALFOY

Draco Malfoy's favorite activity is annoying Harry. They despise each other. Draco is cunning and jealous. He loves nothing more than to see Harry and his friends fail, and tries to make that happen whenever he can.

VERNON, PETUNIA AND DUDLEY DURSLEY

Harry lived with the Durselys for more than ten years. They are all the family he had left after his parents were killed. They dislike Harry and express contempt for magic. Their spoiled son Dudley is Harry's opposite: greedy, unimaginative, and self-centered. The Dursleys mistake prestige for real values.

RUBEUS HAGRID

Hagrid is the gamekeeper at Hogwarts school for wizards. He is a half-giant with long black hair and warm, good-natured eyes. He is well-liked among the students, and trustworthy, although his fondness for alcohol interferes with his judgement. But usually he is a gentle person with a special affection for large and ugly creatures like dragons, monsters of all sorts, and centaurs.

MINERVA MCGONAGALL

Minerva McGonagall is the Deputy Headmistress of Hogwarts, head of the Gryffindor house and teacher of Transfiguration. She wears her black hair pulled back in a bun— a symbol of her strictness. She has the ability to transform herself into many creatures, especially animals. However, she prefers to change into a cat because she has the traits of one.

ALBUS DUMBLEDORE

Albus Dumbledore is the Headmaster at Hogwarts School, the most powerful wizard of all. He has long white hair, a white beard, and dresses in long green or red robes. He is highly-educated, peace-loving and wise. Dark wizards fear his power, even though he uses it in the cause of good.

LORD VOLDEMORT

Lord Voldemort is also called the Dark Lord and fearfully nicknamed "You-know-who." He is a powerful magician of the Dark Magic, eager to wreak havoc on his enemies. He can transform himself into different creatures. His aim is to take over the world. Lord Voldemort is Harry's antagonist.

1997 *Harry Potter and the Philosopher's Stone* was published by Bloomsbury Children's Books in June 1997 to great critical acclaim, and won the Nestlé Smarties Book Prize Gold Medal 9-11 years, the Birmingham Cable Children's Book Award, the Young Telegraph Paperback of the Year, the British Book Awards' Children's Book of the Year and the Sheffield Children's Book Award, and has been nominated for the Guardian Fiction Award and the Carnegie Medal (received 'Commended'). The book has now been sold in fourteen countries.

1999 In 1999, the second title in the series, *Harry Potter and the Chamber of Secrets* (published in Canada by Raincoast Books) won the Nestlé Smarties Book Prize 9-11 years, the Scottish Arts Council Children's Book Award and the British Book Awards' Children's Book of the Year, plus it was nominated for the Whitbread Children's Book of the Year Award, The Sheffield Children's Book Award, and the Guardian Fiction Prize. *Harry Potter and the Philosopher's Stone* made the bestseller lists in both the *New York Times* and the *Wall Street Journal*.

2001 In 2001, Rowling received the Order of the British Empire from the Prince of Wales at at Buckingham Palace.

Aiken, Joan. *The Way to Write for Children*. New York: St. Martin's Press, 1982.

"A Rowling Timeline." Book Magazine.com. May, 2000.
[www.bookmagazine.com/may2000/timeline.html]

"About the Author: J.K. Rowling." Raincoast Kids. (Raincoast Books) No date.
[www.raincoast.com/kidstitles/kidsauthors/PStoneA.html]

Beam, Lindy. "What Shall We Do With Harry?" Focus on the Family. July, 2000.
[www.family.org/pplace/pi/genl/A0008833.html]

Bernstein, Richard. "The Reality of the Fantasy in the Harry Potter Stories." The New York Times. November 30, 1999.
[www.nytimes.com/library/books/113099notebook-potter.html]

Blume, Judy. "Is Harry Potter Evil?" (essay) The New York Times. October 22, 1999.
[www.judyblume.com/articles/harry_potter_oped.html]

Bolonick, Kera. "A List of Their Own." Salon.com. August 16, 2000.
[www.salon.com/mwt/feature/2000/08/16/bestseller/index.html]

"Burden of Proof." (TV interview) 'Harry Potter Book Lawsuit: 'Legend of Rah and Muggles Author Claims Trademark Violation.' CNN.com transcripts. July 5, 2000.
[www.cnn.com/TRANSCRIPTS/0007/05/bp.00.html]

Carvajal, Doreen. "Booksellers Grab a Young Wizard's Cloaktails." The New York Times. February 28, 2000.
[www.nytimes.com/library/books/022800potter-book.html]

Carvajal, Doreen. "Children's Book Casts a Spell over Adults." The New York Times. April 1, 1999.
[www.nytimes.com/library/books/040199potter-book.html]

"Children's Literature: Theme." BBC Knowledge (BBC Online). No date.
[www.bbc.co.uk/knowledge/arts/culturefix/childrensliterature/theme1.shtml]

Cowell, Alan. "All Aboard the Potter Express." The New York Times. July 10, 2000.
[www.nytimes.com/library/books/071000rowling-interview.html]

Cowell, Alan. "Harry Potter Frenzy Continues." The New York Times. July 8, 2000.
[www.nytimes.com/library/books/070700potter-goblet.html]

Cowell, Alan. "Investors and Children Alike Give Rave Reviews to Harry Potter Books." The New York Times. October 18, 1999. [www.nytimes.com/library/books/101899harry-potter.html]

Cowell, Alan. "Publishers Use Secrecy in Harry Potter Promotion." The New York Times. May 22, 2000. [www.nytimes.com/library/books/052200harry-potter.html]

Cowell, Alan. "The Subtlety of Hogwarts? Give a Wizard a Break!" The New York Times. August 12, 2000. [www.nytimes.com/library/books/081200anti-potter.html]

Delfiner, Rita. "Is Harry Potter Too Wicca for Kiddies to Read?" The New York Post. September 26, 2000. [www.cesnur.org/recens/potter_061.htm]

Discussion of *Harry Potter and the Goblet of Fire* between Jodi Kantor and Judith Shulevitz. Slate Archives (online magazine). July 10, 2000. [http://slate.msn.com/code/BookClub/BookClub.asp?Show=7/10/00&idMessage=5648&idBio=183]

Discussion of *Harry Potter and the Sorcerer's Stone* between A.O. Scott and Polly Shulman. Slate Archives (online magazine). August 23, 1999. [http://slate.msn.com//code/BookClub/BookClub.asp?Show=8/23/99&idMessage=3472&idBio=111]

Donahue, Deirdre. "Introducing the Author and the Artist." USA Today. July 10, 2000. [www.usatoday.com/life/enter/books/potter/hp07.htm]

"Elizabeth Goudge (Elizabeth de Beauchamp Goudge) 1900–1984." Advancelit.com. 2001. [www.advancelit.com/authors/elizabeth_goudge.htm]

"Fry's Potter: An Interview With Stephen Fry." Amazon.co.uk. (Amazon books interview) No date. [www.amazon.co.uk/exec/obidos/tg/feature/-/49953/202-6646415-1346236]

Glaister, Dan. "Debut author and Single Mother Sells Children's Book for ƒ 100,000." The Guardian. July 8, 1997. [http://books.guardian.co.uk/departments/childrenandteens/story/0,6000,340888,00.html]

Gleick, Peter H. "Harry Potter, Minus a Certain Flavour." (essay) The New York Times. July 10, 2000. [www.nytimes.com/books/00/07/23/specials/rowling-gleick.html]

Grahame, Kenneth. *The Wind in the Willows*. (online edition from
     The Gutenberg Project) Knowledgerush.com. 2000.
     [www.knowledgerush.com/books/wwill10.html]

Hattenstone, Simone. "Harry, Jessie and Me." The Guardian. July 8, 2000.
     *[http://books.guardian.co.uk/departments/childrenandteens/story/0,6
     000,340844,00.html]*

Hoffman, Jan. "The Magical Voice of Harry Potter and Friends."
     (interview with Jim Dale) The New York Times. July 13, 2000.
     [www.nytimes.com/library/books/071300profile-dale.html]

Hollowell, Lillian. *A Book of Children's Literature*. (3rd ed.) New York:
     Holt, Rinehart & Winston, 1966.]

Hurst, Carol. *Harry Potter and the Sorcerer's Stone* (review). Carol
     Hurst's Children's Literature Site. 1999.
     [http://www.carolhurst.com/titles/harrypotter.html]

Iyer, Pico. "The Playing Fields of Hogwarts." (essay) The New York
     Times. October 10, 1999.
     [www.nytimes.com/books/99/10/10/bookend/bookend.html]

Jerome, Helen M. and Jerome V. Kramer. "Author's Childhood Friend
     Says He Was Inspiration for Harry Potter." Book (online magazine).
     March/April 2000.
     [www.bookmagazine.com/archive/issue9/potter.shtml]

"Jessica Mitford." (profile) Bedford/St. Martin's. 1999.
     [www.bedfordstmartins.com/litlinks/essays/mitford.htm]

"J.K. Rowling Interview." (with Ann-Marie McDonald, CBC Television)
     July 31, 2000.
     [http://www.cbc.ca/programs/sites/hottype_rowlingcomplete.html]

"J. K. Rowling's 5 Favorite Children's Books She Read as a Child."
     (quoting USA Weekend - Nov. 12-14, 1999, pg. 4) Lynchburg Public
     Library (VA). Updated December 12, 2000.
     [www.ci.lynchburg.va.us/publiclibrary/ysrowlingsfavorites.htm]

"J.K. Rowling Reveals Secrets of her Success." USA Today. July 9, 2000.
     [www.usatoday.com/life/enter/books/potter/hp03.htm]

"J.K. Rowling." (profile) Educational Paperback Association. H.W.
     Wilson Company. No date.
     [www.edupaperback.org/authorbios/Rowling_JK.html]

"J.K. Rowling." (profile) Hello! Magazine. 2001.
     [www.hello-magazine.co.uk/profiles/jkrowling/]

"J.K. (Joanne Kathleen) Rowling." (profile) The Guardian. 2001.
[http://books.guardian.co.uk/authors/author/0,5917,412962,00.html]

Jimenez, Betty. "J.K. Rowling Biography." PageWise, Inc. 2001.
[http://gaga.essortment.com/jkrowlingbiogr_reak.htm]

"Jim's Biography." (Jim Dale's homepage) No date.
[www.jim-dale.com/biography.htm]

Johnston, Garth. "Harry Potter Fans Detect Devilish Discrepancy."
Salon.com. July 24, 2000.
[www.salon.com/books/log/2000/07/24/potter/index.html]

Kirkpatrick, David D. "Vanishing Off the Shelves." The New York Times.
July 20, 2000.
[www.nytimes.com/library/books/071000rowling-goblet.html]

Kirkpatrick, David D. "Harry Potter Magic Halts Bedtime for Youngsters."
The New York Times. July 9, 2000.
[www.nytimes.com/library/books/070900potter-goblet.html]

"Last Minute Glitch for Harry?" (reprint from Publishers Weekly)
The New York Times. July 6, 2000.
[www.nytimes.com/books/00/07/02/daily/062900pw-potter-glitches.html]

Levine, Arthur A. "Why I Paid So Much for a Children's Book."
The New York Times. October 13, 1999.
[www.nytimes.com/library/financial/101399manage-levine.html]

Lipson, Eden Ross. "Book's Quirky Hero and Fantasy Win the Young."
The New York Times. July 12, 1999.
[www.nytimes.com/library/books/071299potter-sales.html]

Loer, Stephanie. "Harry Potter is Taking Publishing World by Storm."
The Boston Globe. January 3, 1999.
[www.nbp.org/harry.html]

Lurie, Alison. *The Subversive Power of Children's Literature.* New York:
Little, Brown & Company, 1990.

"Magic, Mystery, and Mayhem: An Interview With J.K. Rowling."
Amazon.com. No date.
[www.amazon.com/exec/obidos/ts/feature/6230/103-1753157-4723035]

Maguire, Gregory. "Lord of the Golden Snitch." The New York Times.
September 5, 1999.
[www.nytimes.com/books/99/09/05/reviews/990905.05maguirt.html]

Maslin, Janet. "At Last, the Wizard Gets Back to School." (review) The New York Times. July 10, 2000.
[www.nytimes.com/library/books/071000rowling-book-review.html]

Maughan, Sannon. "Scholastic Confirms Harry Potter Title and Defends Amazon Policy." (Publishers Weekly reprint) The New York Times. June 27, 2000.
[www.nytimes.com/books/00/06/25/daily/062700pw-potter-title.html]

Maughan, Shannon. "Heads-Up for Harry." Publishers Weekly.com. June 26, 2000.
[www.publishersweekly.com/articles/20000626_87602.asp]

Miller, Laura. "Fans Hate Director Picked for Harry Potter Film." Salon.com. March 30, 2000.
[www.salon.com/directory/topics/harry_potter/index1.html]

Miller, Laura. "Harry Potter Kids Cast." Salon.com. August 22, 2000.
[www.salon.com/books/log/2000/08/22/potter_cast/index.html]

Miller, Laura. "Name, Covers of Harry Potter IV Leaked." Salon.com. June 27, 2000.
[www.salon.com/books/log/2000/06/27/potter_title/index.html]

Miller, Laura. "Pottermania at Midnight." Salon.com. July 8, 2000.
[www.salon.com/books/feature/2000/07/08/potter/index.html]

Nel, Phil. "J.K. Rowling on the Web." Updated April 11, 2001.
[www.ksu.edu/english/nelp/rowling/index.html]

Neumann, Maria. "Harry Potter and the Philosopher's Stone: Why Is This Novel So Popular?" Hausarbeiten.de. April, 2001.
[www.hausarbeiten.de/rd/archiv/anglistik/angl-text10.shtml]

"New Harry Potter Book Announced." (Reuters) The New York Times. June 27, 2000.
[www.nytimes.com/library/books/062800potter-title.html]

"Potter's Author's Content Warning." BBC News. September 27, 2000.
[www.cesnur.org/recens/potter_062.htm]

Reid, T.R. "All Aboard the Publicity Train." The Washington Post. July 9, 2000.
[http://www.washingtonpost.com/ac2/wp-dyn?pagename=article&node=digest&contentId=A7240-2000Jul8

Richards, Linda. "J.K. Rowling." (interview) January Magazine. October 2000.
[www.januarymagazine.com/profiles/jkrowling.html]

Rowling, J. K. "The Not Especially Fascinating Life of J.K. Rowling." Cliphoto.com. No date.
[www.cliphoto.com/potter/rowling.htm]

Roy, Ben. "Wiccans Dispute Potter Claims." Citizen Online-Newfound Area Bureau. October 26, 2000.
[www.cesnur.org/recens/potter_069.htm]

Safire, William. "Besotted With Potter." (essay) The New York Times. January 27, 2000.
[www.nytimes.com/library/opinion/safire/012700safi.html]

Schoefer, Christine. "Harry Potter's Girl Trouble." Salon.com. January 13, 2000.
[www.salon.com/books/feature/2000/01/13/potter/index.html]

Scott, A.O. "The End of Innocence." The New York Times Magazine. July 2, 2000.
[www.nytimes.com/library/magazine/home/20000702mag-waywelivenow.html]

Seaton, Matt. "If I Could Talk to My Mum Again I'd Tell Her I Had a Daughter— and I Wrote Some Books and Guess What Happened?" The Guardian. April 18, 2001.
[http://books.guardian.co.uk/departments/childrenandteens/story/0,6000,474412,00.html]

Slatalla, Michelle. "Waiting for Harry Potter in Long Lines on the Net." (technology) The New York Times. April 27, 2000.
[www.nytimes.com/library/tech/00/04/circuits/articles/27shop.html]

Taylor, Charles. "The Plot Deepens." Salon.com. July 10, 2000.
[www.salon.com/books/review/2000/07/10/potter/index.html]

Taylor, Charles. "This Sorcery Isn't Just for Kids." Salon.com. March 31, 1999.
[www.salon.com/mwt/feature/1999/03/cov_31featurea2.html]

"The Author— J.K. Rowling." Stories from the Web. Birmingham (UK) Library Services. Updated July 13, 2001.
[http://hosted.ukoln.ac.uk/stories/stories/rowling/interview.htm]

"The Three Sites of Exeter." University of Exeter (England). Rough Guide to the University of Exeter. Updated January 12, 2001.
[www.xnet.ex.ac.uk/information/rough-guide/university-history.htm]

"Transcript of J.K. Rowling's Live Interview on Scholastic.com."
Scholastic. October 16, 2000.
[www.scholastic.com/harrypotter/author/transcript2.htm]

"Transcript of J.K. Rowling's Live Interview on Scholastic.com."
Scholastic. February 3, 2000.
[www.scholastic.com/harrypotter/author/transcript1.htm]

"Transcript of J.K. Rowling's Live Interview on Scholastic.com."
Scholastic. March 12, 2001.
[www.scholastic.com/harrypotter/author/transcript3.htm]

"U.S. Author Sues Potter Writer." (the Associated Press) The New York
Times. Marcch 16, 2000.
[www.nytimes.com/library/books/031600potter-suit.html]

Underhill, William. "Harry Potter and the Flight from Reality."
Salon.com. July 5, 2000.
[www.salon.com/mwt/feature/2000/07/05/boarding_school/index.html]

Weeks, Linton. "Muggle Versus Wizard: 'Harry Potter' Crew Sues
Author Who Says Her Ideas Were Lifted." The Washington Post.
March 21, 2001.
[http://washingtonpost.com/wp-dyn/articles/A62378-2001Mar26.html]

Weinraub, Bernard. "Harry Potter Book Becoming a Publishing
Phenomenon." The New York Times. July 3, 2000.
[www.nytimes.com/library/books/070300potter-parties.html]

Weir, Margaret. "Of Magic and Single Motherhood." Salon.com.
March 31, 1999.
[www.salon.com/mwt/feature/1999/03/cov_31featureb.html]

Weisman, Steven R. "A Novel This Is a Midsummer's Night's Dream."
(editorial) The New York Times. July 11, 2000.
[www.nytimes.com/books/00/07/23/specials/rowling-weisman.html]

Wilgoren, Jodi. "Don't Give Us Little Wizards, the Anti-Potter Parents
Cry." The New York Times. November 1, 1999.
[www.nytimes.com/library/books/110199harry-potter.html]

Will, George F. "Harry Potter: A Wizard's Return." The Washington Post.
July 4, 2000.
*[http://www.washingtonpost.com/wp-dyn/opinion/columns/willgeorge/
A43112-2000Jul3.html?GXHC_gx_session_id_FutureTenseContentServer
=503f1fdb192c159d]*

Winerip, Michael. *Harry Potter and the Sorcerer's Stone* (review),
    The New York Times. February 14, 1999.
    [www.nytimes.com/books/99/02/14/reviews/990214.14childrt.html]

Yagel, Denise Oliveri. *Harry Potter and the Sorcerer's Stone* (book
    review). Children's Book Page. ProMotion, Inc. 1998.
    [www.bookpage.com/9810bp/childrens/harry_potter.html]

Harry Potter Fan Club
[http://www.geocities.com/thepottersite/]

Amazon.com's interview with J. K. Rowling
[http://www.amazon.com/exec/obidos/ts/feature/6230/002-2465414-1137813]

Stories on the Web's Interview with J. K. Rowling
[http://hosted.ukoln.ac.uk/stories/stories/rowling/interview.htm]

Kidspeak: a group opposing banning Harry Potter books in schools
[http://www.mugglesforharrypotter.org/]

Judy Blume's article "Is Harry Potter Evil?"
[http://www.judyblume.com/articles/harry_potter_oped.html]

"J.K. Rowling on the Web": Literary Link's comprehensive listing of web pages related to Rowling and her books
[http://www.ksu.edu/english/nelp/weblinks/literary/childrens.html#rowling]

PICTURE CREDITS

page:

6:   Express Newspaper/
      Archive Photos
11: Associated Press, AP
13: Associated Press, AP
16: © Mitchell Gerber/Corbis
26: © Davidson/Corbis
28: Associated Press, AP
35: Associated Press, AP
36: © Tony Arruza/Corbis
41: © Adam Woolfitt/Corbis
44: © AFP/Andrea Renault/
      Corbis
48: © Reuters/Stefan Rousseau/
      Corbis

51: Associated Press, AP
57: Associated Press, AP
58: Associated Press, AP
60: Associated Press, AP
64: © Reuters/Ralph Orlowski/
      Corbis
74: © Reuters/Brad Rickerby/
      Corbis
80: © Reuters/James Morgan/
      Corbis
82: Associated Press, AP
90: Associated Press, AP

cover: Associated Press, AP

CHARLES J. SHIELDS writes from his home near Chicago, Illinois, where he lives with his wife, Guadalupe, an elementary school principal. Shields was chairman of the English Department at Homewood-Flossmoor High School in Flossmoor, Illinois.